ANTHROPOLOGY AND THE COGNITIVE CHALLENGE

In this provocative new study, one of the world's most distinguished anthropologists proposes that an understanding of cognitive science enriches, rather than threatens, the work of social scientists. Maurice Bloch argues for a naturalist approach to social and cultural anthropology, introducing developments in cognitive sciences such as psychology and neurology and exploring the relevance of these developments for central anthropological concerns: the person or the self, cosmology, kinship, memory and globalisation. Opening with an exploration of the history of anthropology, Bloch shows why and how naturalist approaches were abandoned and argues that these once valid reasons are no longer relevant. Bloch then shows how such subjects as the self, memory and the conceptualisation of time benefit from being simultaneously approached with the tools of social and cognitive science. *Anthropology and the Cognitive Challenge* will stimulate fresh debate among scholars and students across a wide range of disciplines.

MAURICE BLOCH, Emeritus Professor of Anthropology at the London School of Economics, is one of the world's leading anthropologists. He has held a number of academic positions at universities around the world and is currently an associate member of the Institut Jean Nicod of the École Normale Supérieure in Paris engaged in an interdisciplinary research project on comparative epistemics funded by the European Science Foundation. He has published widely on his research interests and his work has been translated into twelve languages. He was elected a Fellow of the British Academy in 1990.

Anthropology and the Cognitive Challenge

MAURICE BLOCH
London School of Economics and Political Science

professionals, amateurs or students. Its point is to show why anthropologists cannot avoid many of the questions and findings which have recently concerned the various cognitive sciences. These topics have major implications for all the work anthropologists do, even though this might not be immediately obvious to them. This also is true for some other social scientists, for example, sociologists and historians, and so the argument will be relevant to them also. Whenever in this book I refer to social science it is to all these social sciences that I have in mind. However, the focus will remain with cultural and social anthropology. The book should also be of interest to cognitive scientists if only because it will explain to them the difficulties that their social scientist colleagues have in integrating their work with their practice and theories.

So that the relevant cognitive theories and findings alluded to can be easily comprehensible for those who have no previous acquaintance with the disciplines from which they originate, these will be presented in the type of language which is normally used by those who are more familiar with the vocabulary and the type of rhetoric common in the social sciences.

This book differs from typical introductions to cognitive anthropology. This is because it is addressed to *general* social and cultural anthropologists and other social scientists such as historians and sociologists, especially those who would normally not have a special interest in cognitive issues. Thus, it is not intended as an introduction to the subdiscipline: 'cognitive anthropology'. It is addressed to all, or any, scholars, students or members of the general public, who are concerned with the central issues of social and cultural anthropology and similar social sciences. It does not deal with *a certain class of phenomena*, as would be the case, for example, with a book on the anthropology of religion; instead it consists in a discussion of fundamental theoretical concerns which affect every aspect of social science.

Of course, some of the topics considered here are the same as those which have been discussed by those who identify themselves as 'cognitive anthropologists' and who primarily seek to make a contribution to that sub-discipline, but the difference in the purpose of authors of such books and my intention here is that these scholars seek to carve out a specific field within the larger topic of anthropology. They have often done this by defining areas where the methods of psychological testing, or something like them, could be applied to questions of anthropological interest. Such work is of value and is often undervalued by other anthropologists, partly because the difficulty of the project means that cognitive anthropologists have to deal with limited questions which may appear slight and, partly because, as a result of these same difficulties which restrict the topics addressed, they rarely venture beyond their own culture (see D'Andrade 1995 for an excellent account of this tradition). By contrast with this type of approach, this book is intended as a very general theoretical critique and contribution to the way anthropology and other social sciences usually go about their business, whatever they are talking about and whatever part of the world they are studying. As a result, methodological issues, which so dominate the study of cognition, are not my main concern here, though I hope that the methodological implications of the discussion will be useful for those who want to take them up.

Many cultural and social anthropologists not only omit in their studies to take into account the workings of the mind, they are actively hostile to any attempt to do so. The most familiar, and in some ways superficial, expressed reasons for this distrust are two. Because these objections reappear in different forms, they will be considered more fully and in different ways throughout the book.

The first is that many believe, like the anthropologist Geertz for example, that public symbols and private mental knowledge are completely different phenomena (Geertz 1973: ch. 1). According to such writers, psychologists are concerned with individual phenomena while anthropologists are concerned with shared public cultural phenomena. Consequently, because such anthropologists draw a very sharp contrast between their own subject and psychology, they assume that different methods and different theories are appropriate for the 'different' types of meaning different disciplines study (see Strauss and Quinn 1997: ch. 2). But, in fact, a moment's reflection will reveal that 'meaning' can only signify 'meaning for people'. To talk of, for example, 'the meaning of cultural symbols', as though this could be separated from what these symbols mean, for one or a number of individuals, can never be legitimate. This being so, an absolute distinction between public symbols and private thought becomes unsustainable. For example, if we say that a building like the wailing wall in Jerusalem is an object endowed with great cultural meaning, by such a statement we can only mean that, because of a common education shared by a number of people, this object has the potential to trigger reactions in certain people's minds and associated behaviour. It is important to note that the reactions so triggered are likely to be similar for many people and, indeed, the cause of this similarity is an important subject of study, but this in no way alters the fact that meaning remains simply a feature of individual human minds and is not, to use Durkheim's famous terms, a matter of 'a collective representation'. The representations triggered by the wall are most probably different for Palestinians and Jews, but this is because of the different education, social environment, memories, etc., of the members of the two groups, and, thus, it is not the wall, as such, which has meaning. What is more, it is probable that the reactions triggered by the wall also differ within the group of people who identify themselves as either Palestinians or Jews. In other words, meaning can, in the end, only be an attribute of individual minds; there are no such things as purely 'cultural meanings'. The distinction between psychology and anthropology proposed by certain anthropologists is not based on a distinction of the phenomena studied by the two disciplines. There cannot, therefore, be a legitimate claim that the methods and theories of the one or the other discipline are irrelevant for the understanding of what the other studies, nor that these can be protected from criticisms which come from either side.

The other reason why cultural and social anthropologists often dismiss cognitive considerations is more legitimate. It is because of a more or less explicit fear that in introducing cognitive considerations – which are usually in terms of 'what people are like in general' irrespective of particular historical or cultural contexts – they will fall into a type of error which has dogged the theoretical history of anthropology and which is often labelled *reductionism*. The type of reductionist explanation which anthropologists have in mind is of the kind sometimes employed by, for example, Malinowski when he explained the magical practices of the people of the Trobriand Islands, a culture of the South Pacific which he had so brilliantly studied, as being caused by the need for 'reassurance' (Malinowski 1925: pp. 107ff). What worries most modern anthropologists with this type of 'explanation' is that it is trivial. Trobriand magic may well reassure the Trobriand sailor as he sets out on a perilous expedition. This is quite likely to be the case, but it does not account for what Malinowski suggests it does: that it explains how it has come about that the Trobrianders hold the specific beliefs which lead them to speak the specific spells which Malinowski witnessed. Such a general cause as the need for reassurance cannot account for something as unique as the very particular Trobriand magical practices. At first, the explanation in terms of reassurance sounds very convincing, but this is probably due to an unintentional sleight of hand. In order to make his readers believe that his explanation 'accounts' for the phenomena, Malinowski has to make his readers forget about the particular character of what he is trying to explain, in this case specific Trobriand magical spells, reduce them to such generalities as 'appeals to supernatural forces for protection', a vague characterisation which in no way specifies what is at issue, and, in this way, avoids getting to grips with what he is apparently informing us about but giving us instead something which is an empty tautolology. This is the type of reductionism which anthropologists have rightly learnt to beware of and they therefore are always prone to suspect it when they come across explanations of ethnographic data which are also in such general terms as the 'need for reassurance'. This is what makes many suspicious of explanations of anthropological phenomena in terms of general cognitive human dispositions or mechanisms. The reader of this book should not find cause to suspect the arguments presented here to be guilty of such reductionism.

There are, however, much more vague and general reasons for the aversion to the introduction of a consideration of a subject such as cognitive science within social and cultural anthropology. This hostility is part of the general mistrust of social scientists and natural scientists noted in the first paragraph of this chapter but it is particularly intense in anthropology. Some of these objections have to do with a fear that a naturalist approach to anthropology will lead to unacceptable racist and sexist political positions. That this is not the case will be explained in chapter 2. More fundamental, however, is the fact that the history of the subject has led to a fundamental epistemological revolution concerning what kind of study anthropology is. This history will be considered in chapters 3 and 4 but a few lines are necessary by way of introduction.

Anthropology started off as a natural science and ever since has tried to distance itself from this position. It has moved away from its beginning with ever greater horror as though it was fleeing from a disgraceful yet haunting past. This transformation has been represented in terms of a spurious confrontation between 'nature' and 'culture' in which social and cultural anthropology has declared itself the champion of 'culture' against a 'nature' which includes a consideration of the working of the mind. Social anthropologists have, as a result, seen themselves as studying a self-contained phenomenon, 'culture' or the 'social', which is somehow imagined as existing independently of the human organism.

Such a background is unwelcoming for the reception of an argument such as the one this book will propose. However, what will be argued is that anthropology needs to exorcise its old ghosts by re-examining its history and that, then, the absolute need for a central consideration of cognitive issues will once again become evident.

A claim that the consideration of the working of the mind is necessary for all practitioners of a subject such as anthropology has come to seem bizarre if not dangerous. Even if not categorically opposed to the idea, most anthropologists, sociologists or historians have been quite happy to proceed in their studies without acquainting themselves with such disciplines as cognitive psychology or neurology, if only because these are natural sciences. They may, in the best of cases, recognise that these have a connection with their concerns but they consider this connection none of their business. In any case why, they ask, should they be bullied into acquainting themselves with this area of knowledge when there is so much apparently more relevant work with which they are hardly able to keep up? They will argue that there are many other more 'cultural' disciplines, such as literary studies, traditional philosophy or history, which, because they are more similar in rhetoric, have more genuine claims to be relevant to what anthropologists study. They simply do not have enough time for all of them. Why should the study of cognition have a more imperative claim?

The reason is that cognition *is* different because it is *always* central to what is at issue. This centrality is due to the fact that anthropologists are forced, by the very nature of their subject matter, to 'do cognitive anthropology' all the time. They, like many other social scientists, are 'doing cognitive anthropology' as soon as they claim to represent the knowledge of those they study, as soon as they try to explain the actions of people in terms of that knowledge, as soon as they warn the general public, or each other, of the dangers of ethnocentrism, as soon as they discuss the extent, or the limits, of cultural variability. This is so when, for example, they claim, with writers like Foucault, that there is no such thing as 'human nature' outside a particular historical context, or when they try to explain the mechanisms of social and cultural change as a result of processes such as globalisation, or of the domination of one group of people by others. They involve themselves in cognitive studies when they tell us what people 'are like' through the use of the techniques of ethnographic description and interpretation. All anthropologists and similar social scientists, inevitably, in all their writings, are continually and centrally handling issues concerned with cognition and they are continually using cognitive theories to build the very core of their arguments. However, because anthropologists usually do their 'cognitive anthropology' in an unexamined and unselfconscious fashion, the cognitive theories they actually use are the hazy cognitive theories of folk wisdom, their own and those of the people they study; precisely the kind of theories which the cognitive sciences have so often shown to be misleading. This is why it is necessary for anthropologists to learn to criticise and re-examine these tools which they use with such misleading ease, especially when they are unaware that they are doing any such thing.

An inevitable result of this way of going about things will be that some parts of this book will be negative and cautionary. This will be particularly true of chapters 2 to 5 and parts of chapter 6. Thus, such things will be said as 'beware and be suspicious of anthropologists who, in the very manner with which they write, imply unproblematically that the presence of a way of saying things among a particular group of people means that this is how *those people think* about this matter'; or, as will be discussed in chapter 8, when an anthropologist is talking about 'memory' it is uncertain whether she is referring to what people actually remember or, like the French sociologist Maurice Halbwachs (1950), she is indicating what they can, and do, say about the past when socially suitable occasions crop up.

The negative side of the book

There are three reasons for the negative side of the book. The first is because it is the philosophical and psychological sides of cognitive science that are most useful as a continual criticism of the normal practice of anthropology. The same applies to such disciplines as sociology or history. The point of the book is not to make anthropologists and these other social scientists do different types of things to what they already do, in other words, to make them, as some would have it, into a kind of cognitive psychologist in the field. Rather, it is to make them add a new dimension of caution and awareness to the way they proceed with the tasks they are doing anyway.

The second reason for the cautionary side of the book is that examining critically the history of a discipline such as anthropology enables us to understand why and when certain misleading steers have occurred. As a result of such examination, we can reconsider and possibly free ourselves of directions which have swept us along but which, on reflection, we may realise have been misleading.

The third reason for the critical tone is that we must recognise that the study of cognition is in its infancy and that, as is typical of this stage in the development of a discipline, its greatest successes have consisted in casting doubt on folk wisdom; folk wisdom which is often the indirect product of long abandoned scientific theories. As a result, the cognitive sciences are more certain when telling us what things are not like, than when telling us how things are. This stance may be disappointing, but it is a familiar state of affairs; indeed, it is one in which anthropology often finds itself. After all, what most anthropologists are still most confident about, and most united in claiming, are negative propositions concerning the folk anthropological assumptions which surround us, whether these are found in the press, in everyday conversation, or elsewhere. On the basis of their expertise, anthropologists rightly feel justified in contradicting such commonplace propositions, and the very terms these use, as: 'people with simple technology make less use of abstract concepts', 'the reason for a belief in witchcraft is due to lack of scientific knowledge' or 'primitive people worship mother goddesses'. By contrast, anthropologists are much more tentative than non-anthropologists in offering explanations why certain people have made certain technological advances and others have not, whether the world is becoming more unified culturally, whether all people distinguish between body and mind, whether traditional cultures are more ecologically minded, or why the ancient Jews forbade the eating of pork. This predominantly negative or tentative stance is not a shameful fact that anthropologists and other social scientists have to admit to; it merely shows that the advances in the subject have often consisted in invalidating erroneous folk assumptions and accepting that we know less than we thought we did. The same is true for cognition.

Thus, in the same way, and for the same reason, that anthropologists believe, given the doubts they have been able to cast on what many people think is obvious, it is not acceptable for other disciplines, or practitioners of activities such as politics or the media, to ignore anthropological questionings and blithely proceed on the basis of folk anthropological assumptions about such things as 'a specifically African type of rationality', or primitive 'intuitive feelings for nature', or on 'the instinctive basis of the incest taboo', or the 'impending unification of all human cultures'. It is equally not acceptable for anthropologists to talk about cognition, whether implicitly or explicitly, and ignore cognitive findings, for example, by assuming that words and concepts are equivalent (see chapter 7), or that knowledge can be 'embodied' elsewhere than in the nervous system (see chapter 8), or that our understanding of time was something we obtain entirely from other people around us during early childhood and which can, therefore, vary absolutely from place to place (see chapter 5).

One effect of this book may therefore, in the end, be to make the reader feel that we know even less than we thought we did, that it is even more difficult to explain people's actions than we previously believed, a state of affairs which may be, from a certain point of view, disappointing, but which should also be salutary and constructive.

The constructive side of the book

The more constructive side of the book will be found in parts of chapter 6 to 8. This should be seen as an attempt to understand the relationship between, on the one hand, what people explicitly say in a declarative manner and what they can be observed doing and, on the other, the cognitive mechanisms which cause these practices and actions. This is a distinction which is not normally looked at in the social sciences because it is so often assumed that the two reflect each other. It is an assumption which will be challenged throughout and so too, consequently, will be the status of the ethnography reported by researchers who make this assumption. My intention will not be to dismiss anthropological data which has been so meticulously gathered, but to reconsider what it is about, as will be done in chapter 5.

The reason why things are seen in this undifferentiated way follows directly from the position anthropology has found itself in as a result of taking the side of 'culture' in the imaginary culture/nature wars that the history of the subject has set up. Within such a context, anthropology has to ignore cognitive mechanisms because these are on the outlawed side of 'nature'. It then follows that anthropology cannot distinguish between types of knowledge with different cognitive status, for example, the knowledge which is used in action and second-order meta-representations which are *about* these actions. Admittedly, and as will be discussed in chapter 7, the distinction I am making here is already to be found in the work of Malinowski (1922) and of Bourdieu (1972). However, because these authors were unable or unwilling to make use of the help which is now available from the other cognitive sciences in this matter their insights stopped short. The second part of this book can therefore be seen, in part, as an attempt to pick up where they left off.

The very general stance concerning distinguishing types of meaningful activity and linking these to different cognitive mechanisms leads directly to much more specific discussions where criticism and positive suggestions are intimately linked. For example, it will be argued in chapter 7, that it is a mistake to assume that the meaning of a word can be equated with a concept in the mind of the speaker of a language which uses this word. Thus, a reflection about the relation of vocabulary to the type of categorisation and inference we do actually use to organise our behaviour will be initiated.

Another reason why such an apparently negative discussion is also a constructive one is that it clears the decks for the formulation of better questions and the book will try to formulate these. Criticism thus makes our task more difficult, but it is also likely to make it lead naturally to the formulation of more positive proposals. For example, if, as will be argued in chapter 7, recent work in cognitive psychology suggests that certain concepts are organised around implicit theories rather than in terms of defining characteristics, taking note of this trend will indicate not only a possible criticism of anthropologists who try to define the concepts of the people they study in terms of necessary and sufficient characteristics, but also it will suggest new ways of trying to discover the contents and nature of these concepts. Again, if, as has been argued in recent work, the concept of 'living thing' is above all a matter of people assuming a set of implicit theories, amongst which is the unstated theory that a living thing must have been born as a child of another living thing, then this will suggest a research strategy where the anthropologist attunes herself to trying to pick up actions, statements and attitudes which involve this kind of implicit naïve inferential activity. These she would probably have missed if she believed, like many anthropologists, that concepts are to be understood as hard and fast definitions, primarily used by people as tools to organise classifications, rather like a philatelist classifies stamps by country and date. Chapter 8 on memory will illustrate the position argued for throughout the book, that is taking *together* traditional questions of anthropology and recent advances in the cognitive sciences, in order not only to clarify issues, but also to formulate new potentially fruitful questions.

If this book can be considered as divided between positive and negative arguments, the hinge between these two stances is chapter 6. This chapter examines what many anthropologists consider to be the core contribution of their discipline to science. This contribution consists in a reconsideration of what kind of phenomenon people are, given the fact that they exist within different cultures and societies. It will be shown how the often obscure and always exoticising discussions about what has been variously called the self, the person and the agent in anthropology can be reformulated in a much more straightforward way. This can only be done if, as a first step, we abandon the opposition between 'nature' and 'culture' and view all aspects of what we study within a naturalist framework which focuses on the working of the mind and the body. Then, once this has been done, we place the anthropological discussions within that naturalised framework. We are then able to relate to each other the fundamentally different types of data that social science and cognitive science disciplines have provided. This is the reconciliation this book seeks.

TWO

Innateness and social scientists' fears

Everybody recognises that the way people behave is in terms of how they know things to be. But where does this knowledge come from? How does it develop in the individual? These very general questions are a good beginning for understanding the need for a psychological input to the social sciences since learning, storage and use of this knowledge is *both* a mental and a social process.

There can only be three possible sources to the knowledge held by people. (1) It can come from an innate capacity, transmitted genetically from the parents, which either the child already possesses at birth, or which develops later, as he or she matures, much in the way that boys develop facial hair at adolescence. (2) It can come from the individual learning from the environment as she interacts with it. (3) It can come from learning from other individuals through some process of communication. For any part of knowledge we may be dealing with a combination of all three.

Social and cultural anthropologists, and social scientists in general, tend to favour the third option, to be not very interested in the second and passionately to reject the first. The reasons for this rejection are the subject matter of this and the next two chapters. So, quite apart from a general distrust of anything which they see as coming from the natural sciences, we must first consider the much more specific fear of the genetic determination of culture. This hostility among many social scientists to innatist explanations of human knowledge, although initially understandable and motivated by very good reasons, should, nonetheless, be critically examined and partially overcome.

These fears are of two kinds: the first is linked with the dread of racist or sexist arguments; the second has to do with the uniqueness of human beings among other animals, a uniqueness which makes the social sciences legitimately different from more typical natural sciences such as biology.

This book is centrally concerned with this second reason. It will not deal in detail with the genetically based differences which might exist between individuals, human populations or between the sexes, all of which might be used to legitimate racism or sexism. But, because anxieties linked to this topic affect the attitudes of many social scientists towards the subject of genetic factors having an influence on cognition, it is necessary to deal with the question of racism and sexism quickly, if only to get it out of the way at this early stage.

Does acknowledging a genetic factor in cognition imply racist or sexist beliefs?

Social scientists often associate arguments which explain why people behave in a particular way as the result of their biological inheritance with various forms of racism. They are rightly on their guard against such a danger because totally false, evil and misleading racist arguments have been, and are being used, to justify terrible crimes. Furthermore, in the past such arguments have often originated, been encouraged or simply condoned by the writings of social scientists. The history of anthropology, which will be examined in the next two chapters, is particularly unedifying in this respect, and so it is not surprising that many present-day practitioners are especially touchy about anything which looks like a revival of a shameful past (Stocking 1987). Luckily, straightforward racist anthropology, once common, is, though far from dead, rare nowadays.

Nonetheless, it should be recognised that somewhat less outrageous forms of this type of argument are still very prevalent, especially in those countries where anthropology is closely linked to nationalism, or where intelligence tests have been used uncritically (Cole 1996: pp. 52–7).

In the past, racist arguments have taken the form that such and such racial group is superior or inferior in intelligence or other psychological characteristic. More recently, they have often been presented merely in terms of claims for the unique cultural characteristics of certain groups which are represented as remaining unchanged through long periods of time, irrespective of historical circumstances.

There is usually not the least valid evidence to support a simple genetic basis for the various characteristics in question. We are, most often, actually dealing with pseudo-scientific glosses on long-established prejudices and slanders. There is certainly the possibility that some psychological characteristics are more common within a particular population, however defined, than in another, and that a genetic factor is somehow involved. This, however, in no way justifies racist arguments for at least four reasons.

First, racism, as its name indicates, is about differences between *races*, and the idea of race itself is misleading because the genetic reality is that human beings do not divide up into the type of clear categories with neat biological boundaries which the word implies. Rather, we are dealing with gradual statistical variations in the frequencies of specific genes. Furthermore, the frequency, or otherwise, of particular genes which differ within human populations do not normally differ in unison. If we take the example of genes involved in the ABO blood group, we find that these vary in frequency independently and in a different way from the genes involved in the rhesus blood group. The genetic picture, as far as we know it, does not justify therefore the idea that humankind is divided into distinct or discrete groups.

Secondly, single genes do not normally determine characteristics in a straightforward manner. Usually, it is a combination of many genes, varying independently but interacting together with environmental and developmental factors, which produce the phenomena which affect what individual people are like. This is so for fairly straightforward characteristics such as height or body weight. For the much more complicated phenomena, which vague words like 'intelligence' or 'personality' indicate, the effect of individual genes is even more indirect, not to say obscure. Once again, this complexity, taken together with the facts that different genes vary independently, means that genetic differences do not produce different bounded groups in the human population (Montagu 1942).

Thirdly, there is always as much if not more genetic diversity within populations than between them. Of course, statistical contrasts may be established which distinguish groups one from another. It should be remembered, however, that such contrasts depend on the arbitrary definition of units in the first place and would exist between any arbitrarily defined groups, however distinguished. Thus, although, most probably statistically significant genetic differences affecting the brain exist between, for example, the populations of France and Germany, this would also be the case between the population of northern Germany and northern France taken as a single unit, in contrast to the merged population of southern France plus southern Germany. The point is that the recognition of real contrasts does not legitimately establish the *essential* existence of the units involved.

Fourthly, even if there were marked genetically governed psychological differences which vary systematically between or within populations, this could, of itself, not be an argument for treating people issued from different populations differently. After all, there is no doubt that there is a genetic factor affecting hair colour but nobody suggests that it would be legitimate that people with dark hair be treated differently from those with light hair.

In fact, the fear that simply taking into account genetic factors in cultural and social anthropology will inevitably justify racist or sexist views, and the consequent refusal to even hear them discussed, makes social scientists ignore the very best reasons to refute such views. It is clear that all living members of the species *Homo sapiens* are descended from a small group of fairly genetically homogeneous individuals, who lived at most 200,000 years ago, and it is even quite possible that we are all descendants of a group of 5,000 or so individuals which still remained undifferentiated only 50,000 years ago (Donnelly and Foley 2001). This means that given what we know about the rate of genetic change, there is simply not enough time for very significant intra-species genetic differentiation to have occurred. We are all far far more the same than different. This applies just as much to genetically determined mental characteristics as it does to any other.

Such arguments are also relevant, in a somewhat similar way, to fears that recognising the possibility of psychological differences, which are, either directly or indirectly, due to the different chromosonal make up of males and females, need have sexist implications. The genetic differences between male and female individuals are tiny compared to their similarities and there is, as yet, no incontrovertible evidence that sexual differences have psychological implications. But, even if there were, there would still be wide differences within both sexes and great overlap (Baron-Cohen 2003). And again, as in the case of race, the existence of such differences could not possibly justify discrimination or differential treatment.

To sum up, the recognition of the existence of innate psychological characteristics in humans does not, in the least, commit one to accept the possibility that there are very significant differences of this type, between the different groups of people which we commonly distinguish, or between men and women. Furthermore, even if such variation were shown to exist, the recognition of such a fact would not, *in any way*, imply support for racism or sexism.

In any case, as far as this book is concerned, when the topic of innate psychological characteristics will be discussed here, it will be characteristics of the species *Homo sapiens sapiens* as a whole which are at issue.

Nonetheless, irrelevant, unspoken but understandable fears of racism and sexism are best laid to rest as a preliminary in order that the reader may approach the subject in a more relaxed way.

The significance of cultural knowledge for human beings

The second major reason why social scientists in general, and social and cultural anthropologists in particular, tend to be hostile to suggestions that there might be an innate element to cognition is less obvious than their fear of racism and sexism. It is, however, in many ways, even more fundamental. It has to do with a basic difference between human beings and other animals, a difference which allegedly makes them so unlike, that a reference to the animal nature of people seems simply misleading and threatens the very *raison d'être* of a subject such as social or cultural anthropology which rightly assumes the uniqueness of *Homo sapiens*.

The transmission of information from parents to children, in nearly all living species, is very largely carried by the genetic and environmental factors which have been passed on. This is obviously true of most aspects of bodily characteristics and, for non-human animals, it is also true of most mental characteristics. Migrating birds for instance know how to navigate, not because their parents have taught them, but because their genes have so affected their development that it has made the techniques involved an instinct. This genetic transmission of knowledge is much, much less important for human beings because during the course of evolution we have developed another parallel though not independent mechanism for the transmission of knowledge. People, as opposed to other animals, pass on, one to another, what they know, often orally, or by means of artefacts imbued with meaning, or through other means, such as the type of non-linguistic learning referred to as apprenticeship, or through a number of other ways. All these transmissions are made possible by advanced forms of communication and co-operation unique to humans, of which language is the most obvious and the most important.

Social and cultural anthropologists refer to this handed-on knowledge as culture,[1] though for reasons which will be discussed throughout this book, the word has led to much misunderstanding and will be avoided as much as possible.

This capacity which humans have for passing information one to another, therefore, means that something which is not transmitted by the genetic code nor from the way of acting which the environment encourages can, nevertheless, be transmitted across the generations. Thus, knowledge can endure over much longer periods than the life of any individual, and, in this way, last, though in continually trans- forming configurations, for centuries if not millennia. In this sense, this knowledge is like genetic material, in that it is something which tran- scends the individual biological organism and its individual existence. It is a little like a type of parasite which can continue to exist because its host reproduces also through time, though its basic reproductive mechanisms are different and independent.

What has been called culture is therefore a non-genetic, very long- term flow of information, in continual transformation, made possible by the fact that human beings are different from other animals because they can communicate to each other vast quantities of data, some of which they then may pass on to others.

This flow is what makes history, and no other animals have anything remotely like human history. Because it is not genetically based, the mechanisms of transmission and mutations are quite different in terms of their causes and in terms of their speed. History can change at a rate which is incredibly faster than anything which genetic mutation and selection could produce in a mammal. Thus, if we compare the rabbits of 5,000 years ago with those living in England today, we find

---

[1] The word culture is a difficult one and the cause of much controversy. See for example Kuper 1999. I do not intend to get into such problems here but what has been stated will probably command rough agreement.

that they are practically identical. If, on the other hand, we compare the humans of 5,000 years ago with those of today, even though they will also not be significantly changed genetically, they will, nonetheless be very different beings because history will have fundamentally transformed them. Humans beings have, to a certain extent, escaped the requirements of the time clock built in to the process of natural selection.

The mechanism of continuity and change in history is therefore human communication. Every act of communication can be seen as distinct but it is in fact suspended in a flow. To understand this, it is simplest to look at just one aspect of this flow, the linguistic one. Every new utterance that is spoken is spoken in the way it is because of an incredible number of other sentences spoken before by the person who has uttered it, of other sentences heard by the speaker, of sentences heard and uttered by those who spoke the sentences heard by the original speaker and so on. This is because what one says is always, consciously or unconsciously, in indirect or direct answer to what other people have said to you; it is in relation to the way one has learnt how to say things, and in terms of one's memory of how others and oneself have reacted to what was said. And, of course, these other utterances too, have been shaped by similar conversations and memories, a chain which stretches back and back to the very emergence of *Homo sapiens* and probably before.

And, as if this complex flow was not sufficiently complex in itself, one must remember yet another aspect of human communication which makes it even more fundamentally different from genetic communication. Although every act of communication is inevitably bounded in time and therefore distinct, these units are not normally stored by individuals in the heads of those to whom they have been transmitted as distinct, or even in the form in which they were communicated. Rather, they are reorganised and merged with other previously learnt information and, for the most part, lose all identity as they become part of a greater integrated whole. This process of transformation from the mental to the public and from the distinct to the assimilated and back again gives yet a further twist to historical transformation which again distinguishes it radically from genetic transmission.[2]

Finally, all these facts about the speed of change of human history and about its complexity have yet another, equally fundamental, implication. They explain why there is so much diversity within the human species. This is because since the flows of information are so rapid and cumulative it is easy to see how divergences can become different streams much much faster than genetic differentiation of populations can take place. Of course, the image of streams is somewhat misleading in that these differentiations are never complete or irreversible and mixing between relatively differentiated currents continues to occur at greater or lesser rates. Nonetheless, the differentiation of humans in general, into somewhat distinguishable 'cultures' is a fact and has rightly been seen as a basic legitimation of disciplines such as cultural and social anthropology.

The point of this fairly familiar rehearsal of these fundamental reasons for the immense difference that human history creates is that it makes clear why anthropologists stress that explanations of why people do things in a particular way must always be in terms of the historical and social environment in which they live, in other words of the particular context of the particular stream this long-term differentiated history of communication has created. They are quite right. But their enthusiasm for this fundamental point often unjustifiably leads them to deny the relevance of *any* factor affecting cognition dependent on genetic or environmental factors common to the species.

This denial often takes the form of a kind of plea for a disciplinary apartheid between the life sciences and the cultural sciences. The history

[2] In stressing the importance of taking into account the significance of the passage from the mental to the public I align myself with the position of Sperber (2001) against the formulation of Dawkins (1982) and Dennett (1995) in their discussion of memes; however, in stressing that units of communication lose their identity when stored in the brain I distance myself from the position of all three writers (Bloch 2001).

of anthropological controversies surrounding sex and gender offers an example of this tendency and shows well the unhelpful form this type of discussion often takes. This is all the more so, because one element acting as a driving force behind much of such work is a feminist determination to fight sexism which it is assumed, wrongly, is best defended by emphasising the fact that human beings *completely* construct themselves throughout history and in this way *free* themselves from *any* constraints that might originate in their biological nature.

This kind of extremism has led to the situation we find so often in the social sciences and especially in social and cultural anthropology where anything that seems like an explanation in terms of the characteristics of the species is denounced. This state of affairs is the product of a long and unfortunate intellectual history. As we shall see in the next two chapters, this has much to do with the unfortunate opposition of 'nature' versus 'culture'.

THREE

How anthropology abandoned a naturalist epistemology: a cognitive perspective on the history of anthropology

The purpose of this chapter is to show in more detail how the history of social and cultural anthropology has always involved suppositions and implicit theories about the nature of human mental processes whether the practitioners of these disciplines are aware of this and whether they like the idea or not. This involvement of anthropology with psychological issues is as true of periods when cultural and social anthropologists were most hostile to natural science as when they saw their subject as part of it. Because these largely implicit theories underpin all work in the anthropological disciplines, the effect of not examining them critically is that it leaves us at the mercy of their subterranean determinations.

Probably the most damaging legacy of the lack of examination of the implicit psychological underpinnings of social and cultural anthropology has been that it has transformed what should have been a fruitful controversy about the effects of the specialisation of the human brain on history into a highly misleading and sterile one about whether humans were to be seen as either 'cultural' or 'natural' beings. This opposition still haunts the discipline. What follows is an explanation how this has come about, how it has damaged theoretical reflection and how it can be avoided.

Early evolutionists and naïve naturalism

As an academic subject, anthropology began with a bang during the last two decades of the nineteenth century though at that time social and cultural anthropology were understood as constituent parts of the larger anthropological discipline. What began then was the type of anthropology that became a recognised discipline in universities, principally in Europe and North America, but also in Asia and South America. The dates of the major publications that were to have a subsequent influence are significant since, for the most part, they closely follow on from the publication and the subsequent turmoil caused by the appearance of Darwin's *The Origin of Species* in 1859 and *The Descent of Man* in 1871. It can thus be said that modern academic anthropology is a child of the discovery of the principles of natural selection. The most important founding authors, writers such as Tylor in England and Morgan in the United States, were, by the time of the publication of their major works, admirers of Darwin. Partly because of this genealogy, there is no doubting that for the founders of the subject anthropology was a natural science.

Of course, in the general sense of a science of man, there had been anthropology long before. In looking for the origin of the subject one can go back to the earliest writings we know, certainly back to Greek writers such as Herodotus, or probably before. In this search for predecessors, we might even want to include such works as the book of Genesis. In fact, there probably never has been any group of human beings, literate or otherwise, who did not speculate and form hypotheses about the origin of human beings and the range and causes of diversity among people. Indeed, since the mid-eighteenth century a growing number of books were published which can be seen as the direct forerunners of the great anthropological works which became the foundation of the academic subject. However, in the period following Darwin's demonstration of natural selection, a new and quite different determination is evident in those seeking to establish anthropology in the new kinds of universities that were then being created or revived. It seemed obvious to them that there was a need for an anthropological science. This is evident in the tone and confidence of the publications that followed.

For those who had accepted the revolutionary implications of the demonstration of the existence of a credible mechanism for the origin of species the task of the new science was clear. It was to write the much longer history of mankind which the new evolutionary theory required, not the short history which concerned professional historians, nor that required for the longer, but still clearly much too short, time which the church declared had elapsed since the creation. What was needed was a history that followed the story of mankind from, at least, the time of the emergence of *Homo sapiens*. This history was to be the business of anthropologists and it concerned, at least, several thousand years.[1] Only for the recent past could anthropologists hand over the story to their academic colleagues, the historians, since these, they believed, were only competent for what had happened in relatively modern times when the appearance of writing meant that it was possible to rely on the examination of literary sources.

The job of the anthropologist was to trace that very long history from the early beginnings of mankind up to relatively modern times. One implication of thinking of the Victorian modern as the destination of the journey was very important. Then, and to a certain extent still now, the modern was defined by the technological prowess that had led to ever-greater mastery over nature. This meant that, since anthropology was the study of the long-term history of humans, it seemed natural that it had to be an account of gradual progress. As a result, almost from the birth of the subject, progress became easily amalgamated with the popular images of evolution as caused by natural selection. But, of course, the

---

[1] Even though these early anthropologists believed that the history of mankind was much longer than the theologians had argued, subsequent research has shown that they too greatly underestimated it.

idea of a necessary direction, or order, to evolution, which is implied by the idea of progress, actually runs counter to the most fundamental and most shocking implication of Darwinian evolutionary theory. This rests on the demonstration of the *accidental* nature of what furnishes the raw material for the process and the specialisation of species. The selection of certain characteristics over others is due to a quite different mechanism which, in any case, is also not purposive since within it is not directed in any specific direction. Nevertheless, the false amalgam of progress and evolution was common, as it has been ever since for the general public. Even Darwin himself was sometimes guilty of merging progress with evolution. This amalgam led to an image of the history of life as a progression from lower beings to higher beings, the highest was, of course, *Homo sapiens*. Borrowing this misleading but dominant stance, anthropology was envisaged as having a part to play in the study of a progress which was the continuation of the story that led to the emergence of humans. The job of the anthropologists was understood as taking over the story of the rise to superior states from where the biologists had left off and then to continue the narrative up to the point in time when, with the advent of writing, the historians would take over. The writers who founded the academic subject of anthropology therefore saw themselves as contributing to this greater encompassing project which was the study of evolution/progress. It is not surprising that they are normally, and rightly, called evolutionists.

This period in the history of anthropology has been well studied and documented (See Stocking 1987) but its implication for the development of the understanding of the relation of the psychological, the historical, the biological and the social is less well understood. This is particularly unfortunate since clarifying these relationships explains and renders manageable many misunderstandings. These have recently been made once more acute by the renewal in enthusiasm for evolutionary theory amongst some cognitive scientists which has inevitably been accompanied by the revulsion of most social and cultural anthropologists to any idea of evolution as an explanatory tool for anything they study. The roots of this lie in their previous hostile relation to the evolutionist anthropological writers of the late nineteenth century. As we shall see, the conflicts which these more recent developments have caused have become a major obstacle to any form of intellectual co-operation between those who take a naturalist philosophical stance and those who oppose it.

The evolutionists who founded that anthropology which became cultural and social anthropology were such writers as Lewis Henry Morgan in the United States, Edward Tylor in Great Britain, to name the two most significant ones. They had both made a fundamental choice in how they viewed human evolution. They were monogenists; this meant that they believed that the different groups of humans, present and past, had a single origin, and that they therefore formed a single species. Such a view was far from universal in the 1880s since there were many who believed that mankind was made up of different species with separate origins. By contrast, their opponents, the polygenists, believed people like the Australian Aborigines were not human in the same essential way as Europeans, an argument which was often used to justify slavery or the elimination of native people (Stocking 1987: ch. 3). The polygenists are largely forgotten nowadays since the fossil record and recent DNA studies have shown them to be quite wrong. They are important, however, because their existence at the time when the subject was being established, as well as the subsequent theories which derived from them (Stocking 1968: ch. 3), led the founders of the discipline endlessly, and rightly as it turned out, to stress the essential fundamental unity of mankind, especially in its cognitive aspects. This was a position which they referred in Tylor's phrase as the 'psychic unity of mankind'.

Few, nowadays, would quarrel with the view that there are no fundamental discrete innate psychological differences between the different contemporary groups and varieties of *Homo sapiens*, even though the early writers had very little evidence on which to rely for their assertion. However, the implications of the assumption of 'the psychic unity of

mankind' for evolutionary theory were not very clear to its early proponents. It must mean that the time that has elapsed since the emergence
of *Homo sapiens* until the present, a duration which these early evolutionists could only largely guess at, is insufficient to have brought about
any major psychological genetic variations in the different groups of
descendants of the small band who are the common ancestors of our
species. This conclusion has subsequently been confirmed by the much
more precise dates can now be given for the emergence of *Homo sapiens*
and what we know about the speed of biological evolution. However,
that fact, or in the case of the evolutionary anthropologists, that assumption, had very fundamental implications which they failed to recognise.
It meant that racial variation and the general principle of Darwinian
evolutionary theory were largely irrelevant for explaining the obvious
differentiation that exists within the human family. There could, therefore, be no simple Darwinian explanation in terms of genetic natural
selection for the separation that occurred subsequent to the emergence
of *Homo sapiens*. Whatever caused this diversification must be due to
other factors that have nothing to do with the natural selection of genetic
features. The early evolutionary anthropologists were largely unaware of
this implication of their theory of the psychic unity of mankind, in part
because the basic principles of biological inheritance were unknown to
them. And so the evolutionary anthropologists of the late nineteenth
century ignored the contradictory character of their theories and slid
without much reflection into believing that the story of human history,
posterior to the emergence of *Homo sapiens*, could somehow be told
as though it was a simple continuation of the evolutionary story of the
emergence of mankind as it had been told by Darwin in *The Origin of the
Species.*

Evolutionists, such as Morgan and Tylor, thus made two fundamental
mistakes. The first is that they equated evolution and progress. The
second is that they believed that what had happened in human history
could be accounted for by a story of change motivated by processes

akin to natural selection. The combination of these two mistakes made it possible for the early evolutionists to tell a number of stories that explained post-emergence human history and pre-emergence human history as a unified necessary progression along what was a more or less single line of progress. In the case of Morgan, this was a story based on what he knew from archaeology and ancient history. People had first to be hunters and gatherers, and then they would discover animal husbandry, then agriculture and so on. This fixed succession of changes was necessarily accompanied by associated changes in kinship systems, government and ideas of property. In the case of Tylor, the story was about religion. It concerned the change from simple forms of belief which he called 'animism', that is the belief in the survival of the soul after death, to more complex forms involving belief in Gods. Thus, for both Morgan and Tylor a single evolutionary path had necessarily to be followed by humans everywhere. If this had been true, this would have meant that this path would not only account for the past of mankind, but also predict the future. It is for this reason that such theories were welcomed and adopted by a thinker such as Karl Marx whose purpose was principally political.

The assumptions of the evolutionists had major implications for what they proposed should be the methods to be used by the discipline. The most important of these was the value they accorded to the study of primitives, especially living primitives since the people so labelled by them were seen as fortunate accidents that could be used to yield otherwise missing information about the evolutionary history of the species since the emergence of *Homo sapiens*. For the evolutionists, the people in the world who had not yet reached the 'higher stages' and who were therefore 'left behind' on the inevitable single path to be followed by humanity could be studied as instructive 'fossils' that would furnish information about the early stages of modern humanity.

The problem with this evolutionary story and the method it suggested for the study of the prehistoric past is the uncritically examined notion of the supposed *necessity* for the single linear progression. It was either implied, or clearly stated, by these writers, that this was Darwinian evolution. This, however, was in contradiction to the idea endorsed by Morgan and Tylor that, in the cognitive field at least, because of 'the psychic unity of mankind' evolution was irrelevant since this implied that no significant cognitive development has occurred since the common origin of all humans.

The defence of the anthropological evolutionary writers against the evidence of this contradiction was that, after the emergence of *Homo sapiens*, the mechanism which led to change was not any more the random occurrence and subsequent selection of new heritable genetic traits as in Darwinian theory, but human invention. According to these theories, inventions spread through the population because of their obvious superiority over what had existed before. Then, a ratchet effect meant that one invention became the springboard for the next. For Morgan, everything follows from technological advance. For example, he sees the invention of the plough as a key factor in bringing about changes in human society. But the problem with this sort of reasoning is that inventions and selected heritable genetic traits are not at all the same kind of phenomena, therefore their historical implications are quite different. The very basis of Darwinian theory, at least since Darwinian evolution has merged with modern genetics, is that acquired traits are not inherited. This point is precisely what distinguished Darwin's account from those of other biological evolutionists such as Lamarck.[2] Inventions, on the other hand, are clearly acquired traits. Thus for these to have any significance in human history they must be widely transmitted in ways that have nothing to do with sex and natural reproduction. By making inventions the continuation of natural selection, the anthropological evolutionists were making a category mistake. The

---

[2] Even though Darwin himself may not have been all that clear on this.

repercussion of this error was to be very great. It enabled those who were later rightly to point out what was wrong with this way of thinking to dismiss any and all naturalist approaches in social and cultural anthropology.

What, in fact, the early anthropological evolutionist writers were ignoring was the unique characteristic of the human brain which means that humans are in some key respects quite different from other animals. This is not to say that human uniqueness is unique in the living world as some theologians would have it: all species are unique in their own way and all the unique characteristics of the different kinds of animals and plants that exist have unique implications. All need to be studied, but this is equally true for the uniqueness of humans. This is what the evolutionists forgot. What the early anthropological evolutionist theories obscured were the implications of the specifically unique human characteristic of the human nervous system. In many ways, this is strange since Darwin had been quite clear that the development of the human brain, itself a product of natural selection, had fundamental and dramatic implications for natural history. However, neither he nor the anthropologists who were his contemporaries fully grasped why the capacities of the brain meant that human history was radically different from the history of other living species.

The reason for the lack of continuity between natural selection and human history has been explained again and again, most recently by writers such as Dawkins (1976), Sperber (1985) and Dennet (1995). They point out that the difference is due to the fact that our brain makes us capable of complex communication between individuals who then can store acquired information. This stored acquired information can then be passed on to other individuals, who, in their turn, can pass it on to others, and so on. This transmission process is quite unlike the way genetic information is transmitted. Thus, when evolutionists, such as Morgan, point out the importance of certain inventions for changing the course of history they are quite right but this process must be fundamentally different from Darwinian natural selection. Other animals' cognition is largely to be understood as a dialectic between genetic inheritance and the environment. In some cases, what is learnt from other individuals has some significance in this process. By contrast, human cognition is a process involving the genetic heritage, what we learn from the environment *and* what is communicated to individuals by other individuals. The latter factor is of immense importance. These three sources do not, as we shall see in chapters 6 and 7, remain distinct as we live our lives. However, the fact that what is transmitted from other individuals plays such a great role in making us as we are makes our history a quite different process to the history of other species.

This process of transmission through communication is what makes possible what is commonly called in anthropology 'culture'. The traditional anthropological concept of culture is the idea that people see the world and react to it in terms of what has been transmitted to them by other people with whom they are, or have been, in contact, and that these individuals are or have themselves been in contact with others. The potential implication of this fact is radical and we shall return to it again and again in this book. It means that we can no longer simply assume that we know how a human being will react to this or that situation, or how they will act in the world simply on the basis of the fact that they are human; we must also know where they are situated in the great historical process of human communication and transformation. In a very real way, we are in part made by those with whom we are in contact. This total process is the product of the multitude of contacts which extend in time ever further back. Thus it is better to say we are in part made by history. This history is somewhat different for each one of us since our contacts and the contacts of our contacts are never identical. It is even more different for people who are more distant from each other in space or time. There is thus a sense in saying that, to an extent, there exist no human beings in general but only specific human beings who are made different by their unique culture (Geertz 1973: ch. 2). However, as we shall see in chapter 6, this is in the end misleading. Nonetheless, the fact remains that there cannot be a straightforward single universal history of people in general, as the evolutionists believed.

Every individual is an ever-modifying locus of reception and emission of an extraordinary number of messages which we and others transform, merge and remake within the environment in which we live. Human beings are in continual transformation, are all located in the middle of this maelstrom, which in great part determines their history. It links them differently with a multitude of other people who are their contemporaries and to a multitude of others who have lived before them, in some cases, long before. Every individual is thus in a different location in the middle of a different and continually changing history whose complexity makes it unpredictable.

This complexity, fluidity and unpredictability is what explains why the simple straightforward story that the early anthropological evolutionists were trying to tell was bound to fail. It forgets that another process, quite different from that of genetic natural selection, creates the rapid change and differentiation of human cognition and other natural characteristics. In the great conversation of human culture, every human being is different and every event is unique. There can be no general history of mankind anymore than there can be a general history of the patterns dead leaves make as they fall on a piece of ground. All the grandiose stories the evolutionists concocted have simply been proved wrong and they were bound to be. It is impossible to do what Morgan or Tylor wanted to do, i.e. cut up mankind into groups and then place these groups in a single historical sequence where the 'advancement' of one group is the predicted destiny of another. There are no lasting boundaries within the human conversation; change is rapid and different in every case because the interactions between people are so numerous, so volatile and so extraordinarily complex and because every individual is combining different configurations of factors in the context of unique situations.

Perhaps nothing shows more clearly the difference between human history and the history of other species than their different rates of change. The psychological mechanisms that make history possible bring about change at an incredibly much faster pace than that which occurs for other species. For example, if we compare the Italian hares of today with those of Roman times they are practically identical but if we compare the human population that live in a given territory between Roman times and now there is a fundamental sense in which it can be said that they are not of the same kind. This difference is due to the chaotic accumulation, loss, modification, creation, transformation and merging of knowledge and of accompanying practices which have occurred in the intervening period since the Romans. It seems likely that this rate of cognitive change is ever accelerating.

However, it is important not to forget that the reason why human history has this unpredictable and endlessly differentiated character is not because human beings have somehow become non-biological beings and have escaped natural processes; it is simply that the psychic specialisation of the human brain has introduced for them an equally natural process which is quite different from genetic transmission.

Thus, it turns out that it is because the evolutionists forgot the dramatic psychological implications of what Darwin called 'the Descent of Man' that their theories are unacceptable to modern anthropologists. It is particularly ironic that these enthusiastic followers of Darwin should have ignored these implications of human evolution and the irony was to continue as the critics of evolutionary anthropology thought that they were criticising the character of anthropology as a natural science.

The culturalist reaction

The failings of early anthropological evolutionary theory outlined above is what explains why the reaction against it was so successful.

How anthropology abandoned a naturalist epistemology

The early critics of anthropological evolutionary theory have often been grouped under the label 'diffusionists'. They were a mixed bunch, in many cases motivated by a kind of rearguard fundamentalist religious reaction against all forms of evolutionism. However, the central point that these diffusionists shared was quite straightforward. They stressed the obvious fact that humans borrow from each other. This means that an institution such as kingship, to take one of their favourite examples, need not wait to be rediscovered by a particular group of people as they reach a suitable technological level; it might simply have been borrowed from neighbours irrespective of the 'evolutionary stage' of the borrowers. The reason why this is possible is the process I have been stressing above: the capacities of the human brain for communication and storage. This, of course, is not the way the diffusionists phrased their arguments; instead, what they focussed on was tracing, often imaginary, trajectories around the globe of cultural traits such as megalith building, attributing a supreme value to gold or the idea of a supreme god.

One of the more significant anti-evolutionist diffusionists was the immensely influential American anthropologist Franz Boas, who is considered to be the founder of modern American cultural anthropology (Stocking 1968: ch. 9). His basic theoretical message was that everything about human society was such a muddle that the regular and predictive laws of the evolutionists did not apply to human history. For him, these laws could not possibly explain the complexity that anthropologists found when they were faced with real existing ethnographic situations, and especially when these became known through direct contact with the people concerned. Boas argued that rather than classify different cultures in an overarching system, each culture is best treated as a unique conjuncture of historical events to be appreciated for its own sake. Complexity and unpredictability is what Boas revelled in. He was quite right in pointing out that this is what characterises the human condition and also that this is what the early evolutionists could not account for.

However, one cannot understand the anthropological revolution which Boas's work ultimately brought about simply in theoretical terms. Boas's main concern was fighting racialist thinking that he saw as associated with the attempt to write an evolutionary history of mankind as a whole. When Boas began to write at the very end of the nineteenth century, the mainly liberal implications of the work of such writers as Morgan and Tylor had become replaced by ideologically very different types of evolutionist theories, often polygenist in character, which associated levels of technological sophistication with intellectual potential, which, in turn, was understood as caused by race. Although this association of technological achievement with intellectual potential is certainly also occasionally present in the early anthropological evolutionist, the further association with race is in complete contrast, in spirit at least, with the emphasis on 'the psychic unity of Mankind'.

Those who Boas attacked explained such facts as that the Australian Aborigines were 'still' hunters and gatherers in terms of immutable inherited racial characteristics. The implications of such theories were as much political as they were academic. And the advocates of the kind of evolutionist views which Boas, and subsequently his students, attacked were put forward by writers who were often, and not accidentally, also in favour of the enslavement of 'lower' races, segregation in the United States and restrictions on non-'Aryan' immigrants. In some famous cases, they were members of the Ku Klux Klan. It is not surprising that the Nazis and the eugenics movement subsequently used the work of several of these writers for their own ends (Degler 1991: ch. 8). Against these racist views, Boas stressed the effects of environment and, above all, culture and history. He maintained that this was what created differentiation among humans. These factors were not due to innate biological factors and any suggestion that anything in humans was innate became a target for attack. Ultimately, in the work of Boas's students, this contrast became an opposition between the biologism of evolutionary racists and 'culture' or 'history' which, it was argued, was totally free from anything that could be genetically caused. This type of dichotomous thinking resulted, much to Boas's discomfort, in culture being labelled, by the highly influential anthropologist Kroeber, 'superorganic'. That word has often been said to imply the proposition that humans, as far as mental life was concerned, were not 'natural' but 'cultural'. The theoretical point made by Boas and subsequent writers became merged in an unreasoned way with a philosophical revolution. Thus, anthropologists in the United States were ultimately blindly led via Boas to an epistemologically anti-naturalist philosophy. This was so even though this was not Boas's intention.

The stress on the irrelevance and misleading character of 'biology' and species characteristics for accounting for human history might, at first sight, appear as totally opposed to the argument of this book since its central premise is that we cannot escape taking into account what we know of general human psychology in all types of social and cultural anthropological work. The Boasian legacy thus has led to the contemporary aversion many anthropologists now feel towards 'biology' even though they may have forgotten its origin. However, Boas's reaction to evolutionism and the rhetoric of the diffusionists in general can also be seen in a very different way: as the realisation of the implications of the specialisation of the human brain which creates a unique relation to the passage of time.

The reaction against the kind of evolutionism that was Boas's target was to have long-lasting and fundamental implications. Basically, it was a justified scientific critique of the evolutionists of the time. Politically and morally, it was admirable. But, because it was so clearly scientifically, morally and politically right, because the victory of this point of view had to be fought for so fiercely against powerful evil forces, this has meant that, in reaction, most anthropologists, especially American anthropologists, still now feel, as we saw in chapter 2, that they must continually and incessantly deny any relevance of the neurological bases of culture and of human life in general lest they become tainted by the racism which Boas denounced.

As a result, cultural and social anthropologists who see the struggles surrounding the Boasian position as the very foundation of the type of discipline they practise tend to shudder at any representation of human beings which considers as causative any factors which are 'non-cultural' or 'innate'. This attitude has led to a dualist view of human beings having a body that is the product of biological evolution and which does not concern social and cultural anthropology and a mind that is the product of 'culture' and is 'superorganic'.[3] The opposition between racism and history which lay at the core of Boas's thinking thus rapidly became an opposition between 'culture' and 'nature'. In this perspective, the duty of the contemporary cultural anthropologist appears to many to be to stress the supremacy of 'culture', apparently for theoretical reasons, but, in fact, partly because also of an unstated, and perhaps unconscious, moral and political motivation which is an overhang of an earlier heroic struggle.

The clearest expression of this state of affairs can be seen in the work of a writer such as Margaret Mead who was Boas's most famous follower. In book after book, her message is simple. This is exemplified by a study such as *Sex and Temperament in Three Primitive Societies* (Mead 1935). The moral of the book is that what we (Americans) take as 'natural', i.e. such differences between women and men as unequal involvement in the political and domestic realm, aggressivity or aesthetic refinement, are in fact 'cultural'; they are learnt from 'our' 'culture'. These things are therefore the product of history not of 'nature'. This argument is then demonstrated by pointing out that in 'other' cultures the differentiating characteristics of gender are quite different, or even opposed, to what they are in America. This clear message was so fired by the moral input of the old controversy that it seems to have led Mead to distort the

---

[3] Ironically such writers are often most strident in their condemnation of what they believe is philosophical dualism but for quite different reasons. They stress that dualism is one among many possible cultural representations and that it should not therefore be imposed on the 'other'.

ethnographic cases she used in order to make her point more strongly (Freeman 1983). The political overtones of the claim also explain why her conclusion was so welcomed by those who, like her, were involved in the fight against racism and sexism.

The increasing trend towards the culturalist anthropology that was created in the wake of Boas's influence and especially of his very popular follower Ruth Benedict became even stronger in the kind of anthropology that is often associated with the highly influential anthropology department of the University of Chicago, which stressed the construction of culture around certain key concepts or symbols (Ortner 1973). This soon came to mean that what anthropologists were expected to do was simply to interpret and translate other people's point of view since any generalisation beyond the particular inevitably leads to talk about general human characteristics, in other words to talk about human 'nature'. Such a relativistic stance became the justification for writings that were to be judged in terms of the literary satisfaction of the readers of the ethnographies. This tendency ultimately led to the abandonment of generalising cognitive theory at the level of human nature because this, inevitably, meant taking into account non-cultural elements. Instead, what became valued were particularistic ethnographies of here and there. Such an approach justified the production of highly poetic accounts of ways of 'seeing the world', allegedly found in 'other cultures' (Geertz 1973). These evocations charmed many anthropologists, and even more non-anthropologists, because they encouraged an emphasis of the exotic as a way to mark specificity. The prowess of such literary feats meant that their implications for what they might mean for a theory of human cognition in general were only very occasionally critically examined. The exception were a few writers who were disturbed by the total cognitive and emotional malleability suggested (Bloch 1977; Wikan 1990).

Thus, a fundamental epistemological revolution came about in American anthropology with the main actors seemingly not realising how radical what they were doing was to be interpreted. Others attempting an in-between position have subsequently hardly been referred to. The overwhelming momentum was towards the anti-evolutionary stance that came to dominate and which seems to have obliterated from the disciplinary memory the other theoretical positions that were present in the mid-twentieth century. American anthropology plunged, as if sleep walking, towards abandoning naturalism and simultaneously abandoned any attempt at any form of scientific explanation.

The person who, by contrast with the Americans, was fully explicit about this change was the British anthropologist Evans-Pritchard. His desertion of science was made clear in a dramatic shift away from theories often called 'structural functionalist' and which will be examined in chapter 7. His rejection of earlier positions is expressed in two lectures, one about anthropology and history (1960) and the other about anthropology and religion (1961). In these, he flatly denied that anthropology could ever be a natural science, something which Boas never did. Evans-Pritchard's retraction of his earlier position is best understood as part of a general counter attack on evolutionary ideas in reactionary circles in the England of the 1950s. This was especially evident among those intellectuals who, like Evans-Pritchard himself, were influenced by a renewal of traditional Catholicism and similar forms of religiosity such as the 'Oxford Movement'. In the USA, the shift was more muddled and was associated with Geertz who avoided declaring his position outright and instead claimed to have been influenced by the old nineteenth-century mystico, romantic German philosopher Dilthey and his hermeneutic followers. These totally separated, in a way that has been often refuted, what they called the sciences of 'nature' from the sciences of the 'spirit'. For Geertz, anthropology was to be placed within the vague realm of the sciences of the 'spirit'.

Such an approach inevitably brought about a fundamental change in what anthropologists did. What became valued was ethnography and what practically disappeared was any attempt at generalising about human beings as a species. This caused a theoretical gulf between inter-pretation which involved, as much as possible, adopting the point of view of the people studied, what can be called an internal point of view, and any attempt at general theory about human beings which, inevitably, has to be based on parameters external to any particular group.

Thus, the unchecked tendency to argue that all systems of represen-tations are unique and that, because of this, no systematic explanations of their occurrence is either possible or desirable increased still further. This finally manifested itself in the varied tendencies that became known as 'post-modernism', a trend that, until recently, was highly influential in many anthropology departments. Post-modernism consisted of an amal-gam of approaches coming from different sources outside anthropology that all took as their starting position the rejection of what was called 'grand theory', but which was focalised on Marxist evolutionary theory. The rejection of specific grand theories then became a rejection of the very attempt at science. In anthropology, the theories that were aimed at were more specifically and inevitably the anthropological evolutionary theories and they were endlessly and repeatedly refuted, as if they were still current. By contrast, post-modernism emphasised the uncertainty of knowledge, especially scientific knowledge, and how cultural context created the appearance of misleading certainties. Thus, although the post-modernists thought of themselves differently, their approach can be seen as simply yet a further extreme step in the stress of the supremacy of 'culture' and its absolute freedom of any naturalist constraints. This is why no doubt it appealed so much to many professional anthropol-ogists since it was merely the rephrasing of a position which they had adopted without much self-awareness in the wake of the Boasian critique of evolutionism.

The type of arguments typically used by the post-modernists often go under the label of deconstruction, a term made popular by the French philosopher Derrida in the 1960's. Although what he argued was quite revolutionary for his discipline it reappeared, in the hands of anthropologists, as merely a restatement of the Boasian point about the specificity of cultures. For the anthropological post-modernists, the terms we use, which we mistakenly might think of as giving direct access to the world, are merely the product of a multitude of contradictory cultural assumptions. In other words, like Margaret Mead had argued, we should show that what scientists take as natural is in fact cultural.

FOUR

The nature/culture wars

The anthropological stress on the fact that humans live within a culturally and therefore historically constructed world was justified by the rhetorical trick of continually reiterating the refutation of the errors of early evolutionists. The constructivist claim then appears as the child of the old controversy but, left at that, it also automatically raises difficult problems, both theoretical and methodological. These problems have been pointed out, sometimes very emphatically, most often by researchers with a natural science background. This fact has meant that the criticisms of the culturalist turn have themselves been caught just as much within a nature/culture dichotomy.

The theoretical problem of the culturalists has recently been reformulated in a particularly clear way by the psychologist Steven Pinker as it relates to the mind (Pinker 2002). He convincingly argues that if we live in completely historically or culturally constructed worlds, this would mean that these would vary totally from culture to culture. Strange implications of such a position would then inevitably follow. First of all, it would be impossible to say anything general about the human mind and so psychology as a unified science, in spite of its apparent advances, would actually be a waste of time. Secondly, it would mean that humans are totally and absolutely different from other living species because, according to such a theory, humans are born without *any* cognitive predispositions. If they were, then the idea of total cultural construction would have to be severely qualified since the mind would be constrained by these predispositions.

Such a position would seem a negation of the continuity between humans and other animals that Darwinian theory has made almost universally accepted. This is because there is no doubt that other animals, such as a horse for example, and probably all non-human primates, are born with hard wired mechanisms which control the general lines of the conceptualisation of the environment by the individual. Thus, to return to the example of the horse, the newborn offspring knows what plants to eat immediately after birth and does not need to learn this. Similarly, it instinctively knows who its mother is. It has even been suggested, with a good deal of evidence, that animals such as baboons know in some way the genetic kinship links that exist between them and many other more remote individuals (Cheney and Sefarth 2007). Thus, if we humans had to learn everything we know from others and if human cognition was simply a product of 'culture' and unique histories, then a dramatic and total break would have occurred at a certain time in human evolution which would have made our species totally discontinuous with our pre-sapiens ancestors. A moment's thought makes such an event totally unlikely and, in any case, the fossil record, such as it is, tells a gradual story of humanisation.

From the point of view of natural history, the emphasis on absolute cultural construction which we find often in modern social and cultural anthropology seems highly improbable. And, since the history of the subject has been a kind of mock duel between 'nature' and 'culture', it is not surprising that the reaction to such an unlikely story has been anti-'culture'. Thus it is in line with the rhetorically dichotomous character of the arguments.

Nothing illustrates this total confrontation better than discussions concerning kinship. It is not surprising that the topic of kinship should have been a chosen battle ground for both sides. For the biologist kinship was seen as an obvious place where one could expect continuity between humans and other animals. On the other hand, anthropologists, especially social anthropologists, saw kinship studies as the core of their subject. Originally what was stressed was that kinship systems demonstrated variation within a general framework, sometimes envisaged in evolutionary terms, with some systems being labelled as more 'primitive' than others (Morgan 1871) and sometimes envisaged as a limited set of alternatives constrained by the practical possibilities of social organisation (Radcliffe-Brown and Forde 1950). However, as time passed, and in line with the ever-greater stress on the 'construction' of human cognition as created by history and culture, the orthodox anthropological emphasis moved to underlining how varied, and even incommensurate, the systems that had been called kinship were. Ultimately, it was argued that kinship relations were not affected in any way by genetic closeness, even in the case of mother–child relations (Needham 1971; Schneider 1984).

Meanwhile, on the other side of the battle ground an opposite movement was taking place. With the reinvigoration of Darwinian ideas that took place in the 1960s, a new kind of theory developed. This theory was labelled socio-biology. It argued that the social organisation of animals was both the product and a factor in natural selection which at that time was being redefined more precisely. This redefinition involved arguing that what was selected for by natural selection was not particularly fit individuals but simply the production of more viable offspring. The socio-biologists argued that systems of social organisation in living species were to be seen as devices for this in the same way as are anatomic features. In this vein, in a very widely read book called *Sociobiology*, the most well-known proponent of this theory, E. O. Wilson, argued that human society was also to be explained as a system made by natural selection and explicable as a device for the greatest number of viable offsprings (Wilson 1975).

With this theoretical framework, Wilson was able to argue human kinship systems were to be understood in this way. This universal and single cause, according to him, explains what he saw as recurrent aspects such as incest rules. He saw these merely as devices for ensuring that human offsprings were less affected by possible dangerous mutations that could lead to hereditary diseases. An inevitable inference from this type of argument is that all human kinship systems are basically the same since they are created in order to fulfil the same purpose. Furthermore, it was argued that, since the mechanism that caused these systems was long-term natural selection and that kinship studies had nothing to do with explicit knowledge learnt from others during the course of history, people acted according to the principles of kinship as a result of instinctive, and therefore sub-conscious, motivation.

Such a conclusion is in total opposition to what social and cultural anthropologists know of the people they study since these are quite able to express the rights and wrongs of actions in relation to kinship and to enforce the rules involved. The actors of kinship do not follow some kind of knee-jerk instinct as would be implied by the socio-biologist argu-ments. It is therefore not surprising that anthropologists' response to the biologist Wilson trespassing in the very area that they considered as their speciality was extremely hostile. This hostility was clearly formulated in a small book by Marshall Sahlins, *The Uses of Abuses of Biology* (Sahlins 1977).

As a first step in his discussion, Sahlins identifies socio-biology with eugenics, a pre-Second World War movement which had tried to formu-late policies to improve and control the randomness of human repro-duction. Eugenics took a variety of forms and in its worst guise became the basis of Nazi-type programmes for the elimination of what some eugenists saw as inferior or deficient forms of humanity. The association of eugenics with extreme forms of racism was real enough, although it is misleading to assume that all eugenists endorsed this type of programme. However, Sahlins's identification of socio-biology with eugenics is very revealing. This is because eugenics had been one of Boas's main targets in his fight against racism. The resurrection of the controversy meant that the old battle lines which had seen the birth of American cultural anthropology were once more reconstituted in their original form made more urgent by the memories of Nazi atrocities. As a result, socio-biology became something horrible for many cultural and social anthropologists, something against which they felt it was their moral and political duty to fight, even though they often had little idea what the theory proposed.

Against Wilson, Sahlins's book quite rightly argued that kinship systems do not exactly reflect biological closeness and they, therefore, cannot possibly be straightforward products of selected mechanisms simply adapted for gene reproduction. For example, there are many kinship systems where some first cousins are considered preferred spouses while other, equally genetically close, first cousins are strictly forbidden. Sahlins points out that such a fact obviously cannot be simply explained by a mono causal mechanism based on genetic closeness. Kinship systems are very varied and therefore cannot be caused simply by human-wide necessary and sufficient innate predispositions. The variation in kinship systems that anthropology has revealed cannot be ignored, as Wilson had argued in order to deal with such objections, by proposing that such variations are merely superficial unimportant fluff covering up a universal base. Sahlins shows that variation is present in *all* aspects of kinship systems.

In the end, the Sahlins/Wilson controversy seems to have generated more heat than light. This is not entirely the fault of the protagonists who are in several places more moderate than they appear at first. However, the effect of the controversy on both sides has been to leave behind a memory and an environment of conflict and misrepresentation. The old Boasian debate was revived as it has been again and again. It has left a situation where scholars have felt that they have to choose between 'nature' and 'culture' as though these were alternatives and social and cultural anthropologists have felt that they must choose 'culture' and oppose 'nature'.

The splitters

The Sahlins argument was an almost knee-jerk reaction to the familiar mistakes of the eugenicists and socio-biologists. It was given urgency because of the dangers such arguments had entailed. Once again and, quite predictably, this culturalist position, and others like it, also engendered the opposite response. After the passage of a little time, however, an intermediate position developed. In the book by Pinker, already referred to, and to which I shall return, we find an illustration of this position (Pinker 2002). Pinker concludes his book with a list of cultural 'universals' borrowed from Donald Brown. The implication of this is part of a reassertion of the socio-biological claim that there are some elements in human cognition which are isolated from the historical process of culture and are therefore shared by all healthy human beings. This also implies that there are other elements which are malleable and therefore vary from place to place and moment to moment. As will be discussed below, such a division cannot be maintained but what lies behind the wish to claim the existence of cultural universals is quite understandable. It is the fact, obvious to those with experience of different types of people, especially most social and cultural anthropologists, that when away from the heat of such controversies as the Wilson/Sahlins confrontation, it is clear that all human beings are, in many respects, very similar. On the other hand, the fact of variation not based on genetically inherited characteristics is also obvious. This recognition is what led writers such as Pinker to want to split human cognition into natural, hard wired elements, common to the species as a whole, and other elements which are the product of history and are therefore variable.

Sahlins's arguments not only made their mark among social and cultural anthropologists who, in any case, were mostly already on his side, but, interestingly, also among some biologists who took on board his main points but who reinterpreted them in a way reminiscent of the criticisms made of the anthropological evolutionists by the diffusionists. Such authors recognised that human knowledge could not be a mere epiphenomenon of innate dispositions. This was because of the dramatic and revolutionary implications of the human brain and the way it makes possible the transmission of information between individuals.

Such a position was clearly formulated by the biologist Richard Dawkins in his theory of memes, which is best understood as an acceptance by a biologist of most of the criticisms of the socio-biologists made by Sahlins. In a famous book, which popularised the new idea that natural selection operated at the level of genes rather than at the level of the whole organism (Dawkins 1976), Dawkins added a final chapter on human culture. This implicitly criticised the socio-biologists from a Boasian point of view. Dawkins insisted that human culture could not be explained as a response to genetically driven natural selection but had to be explained by a radically different mechanism which the specialisation of the human brain had made possible. While bodily traits were transmitted by genes between individuals, culture was transmitted between individuals through communication in units that he called 'memes'. The word was intended to point to some formal similarities between genes and memes. These need not concern us here. More relevant is Dawkins's argument that with the advent of the modern human brain, cognitive processes are fundamentally different from what they are for other animals. Memes, he argued, are units of culture which are communicated from one individual to another and then passed on further, again and again, so that they occur frequently within a given human population. The totality of memes that an individual retains in his memory is, for Dawkins, rather like the totality of genes contained in the complete genome of the individual. According to this theory, the collection of genes, given the environment, determines some aspects of the individual; the collection of memes, given the environment, determines the other aspects. Unlike other animals who only pass on information from parent to offspring via their genes, humans are the heirs of a system of double inheritance. Some information is transmitted to them once and for all via their genes; this is relevant for such things as bodily characteristics. On the other hand, some information is transmitted via memes, not once but continually. This comes not only from their parents but also from a multitude of other individuals throughout the offsprings' lives. These are relevant for the knowledge their brain will contain. The idea of memes was greeted enthusiastically by a number of cognitive scientists who through this unlikely route realised for the first time the power of Boas's and Sahlins's anti-evolutionist points. For example, the philosopher Daniel Dennett took up Dawkins's idea and developed it into a full theory of culture as a historical process, stressing, like the anthropologists had done, that this could not be explained directly in terms of the genetic dispositions of humans as had been done by the socio-biologists (Dennett 1995). In spite of gaining numerous adherents, the idea of memes is open to many objections, the most obvious of which is that human knowledge is not made up of a collection of distinct bits or memes (Bloch 2001). On the other hand, it is understandable that it should have been welcomed among biologists since it clarified in a language they understood the old anthropological point about the uniqueness of the phenomenon of human culture and of its historical potential. In the biologists' formulation, however, this realisation did not involve, as it had implicitly done for Sahlins, a general negation of a naturalist approach to our species.

However, the main limitation of the theory is that the meme/gene opposition is as caught up in the misleading categorical opposition of 'nature' and 'culture' which had characterised the history of anthropology. Rather in the way that the hostile reaction to eugenics had ultimately made Boas's theory of culture 'superorganic', so meme theory, in its reaction to socio-biology, made meme creation and transmission totally unrelated to the actual biological individual in the process of life. The theory took into account the 'natural' and the 'cultural' but it separated them in a new theoretical *apartheid*.

The construction of this unbridgeable dichotomy gets further specification in the work of a number of other writers who, like Dawkins, have adopted a research posture which they have labelled co-evolution. The term originally applied to studies of the way when during the course of natural history, different species – orchids and bees, for example – evolve independently but in interrelation. This idea was then used for understanding the 'co-evolution' of culture and of the human genome (Durham 1991). Like Dawkins, a writer such as Durham recognises that human genetics and knowledge are governed by quite different processes and he stresses how the two processes interact and affect each other while remaining independent. There is much to be gained from such an approach, but it is also misleading in that the interaction is never thought of as a unified process. It is as if culture and genetics were, as in the original use of the term co-evolution, distinct different species. In reality, when thinking of human beings we are dealing with a single process occurring within a single organism. 'Culture' and 'nature' may be distinguishable analytically but it is important not to mistake the heuristic separation for an empirical one.

A number of other writers have also tried to account for the co-occurrence of genetic and cultural processes by splitting what they consider comes from one side or the other. These proposals vary but, in some cases, they have also included suggestions how the two categories relate to each other. Whatever failings these attempts at splitting may have had, it is nonetheless clear that the very attempt at combination has moved the anthropological reflection forward.

It is no accident that, at first, the 'splitters' were mainly European rather than North American. As will be explained in chapter 7, the nature/culture wars have not had the same dramatic resonances on this side of the Atlantic as in the USA. For writers such as Dawkins and Durham, it has been clear that there is some truth in both sides of the argument. But the problem that these splitters faced was how to put the opposing sides together. The splitters discussed above mainly come from among biologists who had been finally convinced by the arguments of the anti-socio-biologists. However, some of the most influential splitters have come from social and cultural anthropology.

Structuralism and transformational grammar

One of these is the French anthropologist Claude Lévi-Strauss. He is the first of the modern anthropologists to consider seriously the necessity of taking into account the full implications of the functioning of the mind when dealing with the type of data that social and cultural anthropologists usually deal with.

Lévi-Strauss has always been a maverick among anthropologists and this has much to do with the way he seems to have almost stumbled into the subject during the Second World War. He was not trained in any of the more policed traditions of the main anthropology departments but he built up his early knowledge from rather eclectic readings he picked up because they caught his eye. However, by the mid-forties in New York, he had rejoined the academic mainstream and soon became fascinated by all types of ethnography, especially the somewhat undigested data that had been produced by the Bureau of American Ethnology of the Smithsonian Institution. His interests in related subjects continued to flourish, however, and he ranged far and wide, especially, very significantly, towards linguistics.

American linguistics at the time was dominated by a theory that went under the name of structural linguistics. Structural linguistics was created by the coming together of somewhat different studies concerned with a variety of levels of language ranging from semantics, grammar and phonetics. What united the various approaches to these different levels was the emphasis on structure. This is best exemplified at the phonetic level, at which structural theory is most illuminating. The particular theory of language sounds that was influential in structural linguistics became known as the phoneme theory. It had been developed by scholars from

phonemes by means of strings of binary oppositions was reminiscent of the way the computers of their time worked. Both used digitalised information as their operating system. This identity of the ways of working of language and of 'thinking machines' was particularly significant for Lévi-Strauss as it was for a number of other scientists. The idea became common at the time that, since computers were machines that could perform operations similar to those performed by the human brain, then it followed that the way these machines worked was probably also a good guide to the way the brain *actually* worked. These series of inferences enabled Lévi-Strauss to postulate that the structure of the phoneme system was no accident; it was like that because phonemes were used by, and were products of, the human brain. The phonemic system *had* to be organised in this way because it was operated by the functioning of the brain.

But, if that argument was right, so reasoned Lévi-Strauss, it also must apply to all information systems used by human brains. This hypothesis was to be the basis of the next and most significant step in Lévi-Strauss's reasoning: it meant that since culture was another of these systems used and created by the human brain, it followed that it had also to be structured in the same way as language or, more specifically, phonemes.

The assumption that culture had to be structured according to universal characteristics of human psychology became the basis of Lévi-Strauss's anthropology and for him it defined the job of the anthropologist. This task was, above all, to demonstrate the existence of structures underlying cultural material. According to him, these structures had a universal basis; this was because they were products of the brain, but the content they structured, specific cultural material, was irreducibly unique. These were the product of the Boasian historical process. Facts about the brain in general had nothing specific to tell us about these except as an explanation of the way they were organised. This was rather like the numbering system of a library that tells nothing about the content of the books but helps us to find them. Lévi-Strauss's approach, therefore, at the epistemological level at least apparently fulfils exactly what this book calls for: an approach integrating the cognitive sciences and ethnography without running the risk of reductionism by ignoring the particularism of each case. Given the level of knowledge of the working of the mind available at the time he formulated his ideas, structural anthropology promised the real possibility of overcoming the barriers that had grown up between the natural and the social sciences. It was a naturalistic approach that did not ignore the specificities created by history.

And there was a further reason to hope that this might come about. This was the striking parallel between the Lévi-Sraussian theory and that of the founder of developmental cognitive psychology, Jean Piaget. Piaget himself recognised this convergence and hoped that it would bring about a rapprochement between his work and that of social scientists such as Lévi-Strauss (Piaget 1968). For Piaget, it was structuralism that was to bring them together since he had also stressed structuring as a key element in child development. According to Piaget, cognitive development in the child was a process of organising and equilibrating ever more information. Thus the two theories seemed to complement each other very well. What was missing in Lévi-Strauss's work was an understanding of the way the individual built up structures out of experience and did not just receive structures from others, while what was missing in Piaget's work was an understanding that the structures the adult held in his brain had already come in part ready made via human communication.

Unfortunately, the grand structuralist project did not get very far. Piaget's theory, for reasons that will be discussed below, came under serious challenge, while Lévi-Strauss himself, after having laid out the theoretical basis for his structural anthropology, directed his energies to demonstrating structures in vast bodies of ethnography, often in a somewhat idiosyncratic fashion, rather than in developing his earlier theoretical insights. His followers, also, either engaged in this non-theoretical direction or ignored what had been the original motivation that had lain behind structural anthropology. The reason for this was that these

followers and students, probably because they came from more traditional anthropological backgrounds than Lévi-Strauss himself, brought
with them the old suspicions against any attempt to link any aspect of
'culture' to human biology and psychology (Sperber 1982: ch. 3).

One of the effects, or perhaps the cause, of Lévi-Strauss's lack of follow through of his fundamental theory was that he never felt it necessary
to take into account the major developments in cognitive science that
occurred in the 1960s. These should have shaken the theoretical underpinnings of structural anthropology. However, this type of change in fact
occurred instead *outside* anthropology in linguistics and cognitive science
and was first associated with the criticisms that Noam Chomsky directed
against structural linguistics, precisely the theory where Lévi-Strauss had
sought inspiration.

What Chomsky criticised was the uncertain status attributed to the
'structures' of the structural linguists, especially in the field of grammar.
He then went on to point out the lack of a clear story showing how
these structures, and language in general, could be learnt with the ease
with which they actually are. Chomsky argued that any theory of language
must be compatible with a credible developmental story. In what became
a famous confrontation with Piaget (but it could just as easily have taken
place with Lévi-Strauss had he been present), Chomsky argued that it
was impossible for the individual child to construct grammar by simply
listening to others and then elaborating ever more complex structures
from a zero starting point (Fodor 1980). Piaget had hypothesised a process
by which a child learns a language which just could not occur at the speed
at which it did happen. The only possibility for accounting for the rapidity
of language learning by the young child was that humans were born
with a part of their brain already dedicated for grammar. This language
module, or modules, as they became known, must contain a universal
grammar, already inscribed. This then could be used by the child as a
basis from which to learn the specific grammar of the specific language
into which she was brought up. Only given an innate predisposition,

Chomsky argued, was the universal human feat of language learning possible.

At first sight, such a theory does not seem so dissimilar to the general theory of structural anthropology. Both posit a universal feature of the human mind, in the case of Lévi-Strauss, a universal structuring capacity, in the case of Chomsky, a universal language faculty. In both cases, the universal element then allows for the specific and great variation that one finds in the empirical world, whether this be in the field of language or of culture.

However, this similarity hides great differences. First, Chomskian linguistics does not argue for a *general* characteristic of the mind that could be used for any and all domain of information as did structural anthropology. Instead, it argues that a part of the nervous system is specialised for language and only for language. One of the obvious consequences of this is that the part of Lévi-Strauss's theory that assumes that what goes for language must also necessarily go for culture in general becomes untenable. For Chomsky the mental mechanisms that enable us to use and learn language are special.

Secondly, although Lévi-Strauss makes room for the brain as a biological mechanism which needs to be understood by social and cultural anthropologists because it structures cultural information, he is at the same time too wary of possible reductionism. For him, the structuring capacity tells us *nothing* about the content of what is structured. For him the content of 'culture' is, as it is for Boas and his followers, entirely the product of a particularistic cultural history. On the other hand, Chomskian linguistics argues that the language-structuring capacity of the human brain does, to an extent, determine all natural languages at a deep level. For Chomsky, although at the surface human languages seem to have different structures, there is a deep level where all human languages are the same. This deep structure generates only a limited number of possible surface grammars which all bear its mark. Thus, Chomskian theory proposes a necessary determined element in the surface form of the language though this is not sufficient to explain the way any particular human language is.

Thirdly, there is a further aspect that is common to Piagetian psychology, Lévi-Straussian structuralism and meme theory but which is fundamentally challenged by the full implications of Chomsky's theory. All these earlier positions implicitly, though never explicitly, seem to suggest that the human child at birth is born with a mind empty of content and that this empty mind is then only gradually filled with whatever it learns from outside, whether this comes from the environment or from other people. This is the theory for which Pinker gave the old philosophical label of *tabula rasa* or the 'blank slate' on which information is then to be inscribed. This implicit position is of course shared with the cultural anthropologists who followed on from Boas (Bloch 1985; Tooby and Cosmides 1992; Pinker 2002).

The evolutionary implications of the difference between viewing the mind as a blank slate or as already predisposed for certain types of information could not be more fundamental.

Towards a unified processual perspective

Modular theory had its origins in the Chomskian revolution in linguistics and, although Chomsky himself limited his claims to language, the implications for child cognitive development in general rapidly became evident. The idea that a part of the mind, a module, to use the common term for this, is dedicated to the specific purposes of language led a number of other cognitive scientists to wonder whether there are not other modules of a similar sort, in other words, other parts of the brain dedicated to handle specific domains This suggestion became more probable as a result of a whole set of psychological experiments which clearly demonstrated that very young infants already possess sophisticated understandings of the world. These contradicted the notion of the blank slate implicit in the writings of many of the authors so far considered. Infants' capacity for recognising faces is such a case. A child a few hours old is not stopped from recognising its mother, even though she had previously left her hair loose, and had subsequently put her hair up in a bun (Johnson 1988). Recognising that she is the same person involves identifying a single individual in spite of the fact that the empirical phenomenon, the face, is continually changing from moment to moment. This is an amazing feat that the newborn achieves very soon after birth. It is therefore difficult to believe that this capacity could have been learnt from scratch in a few hours. In any case, much new neurological work seems to show that certain areas of the brain are, in modular fashion, dedicated to this task. Again, experimental work on young children seems to indicate pre-inscribed predispositions of our basic understanding of the material world in specific ways. Very very young infants seem to possess knowledge of the basic laws of physics (Spelke 1988). For example, they seem to understand that one solid cannot go through another long before they could have discovered this through experience. This suggests a module for 'naïve physics'. In similar ways, quite a number of other different modules have been suggested on the basis of experimental work. The most likely candidates would be those that would involve innate predispositions for the understanding of biology, of social relations and, above all, a 'naïve psychology' module. This 'naïve psychology' concerns the ability to read the minds of our fellow human beings. Understanding that people have a mind in terms of which they act is an amazing feat that recent experimental work shows develops in normal human infants at an extremely young age (Baillargeon, Scott and He 2010). Once again, the complexity of the tasks that the child masters at the early age at which it is successfully achieved suggests an innate predisposition which is best explained by the existence of a dedicated part of the brain specially designed to do the job. Indeed, recent neurological work suggests that this is indeed the case (Farrer and Frith 2002).

The theories about language that originally came from Chomsky's work have thus had dramatic general implications for our concept of what it is to be human. Clearly, much of the way we see the world, ourselves and others, is determined by the general characteristics of the species to which we belong. Such a revolution in thinking about human knowledge could not but ultimately have an effect on anthropology. Structural anthropology had brought back the mind into anthropology but it had done so minimally, not really upsetting the consensus that had grown up in the wake of Boas's theoretical stance. Indeed, how little Lévi-Strauss's theory changed the anthropological consensus can be seen when we consider what it means in evolutionary terms. As was the case in the more traditional approaches, the human mind of structural anthropology is understood as absolutely different from that of other animals. This is because, while no one doubts that animals are born with considerable innate knowledge about such things as what food to eat and what predator to fear, structural anthropology assumes that humans, apart from the fact that they possess a structuring capacity, are assumed to know nothing at birth and have to learn whatever they will come to know, either from the interface with the world or from other members of the species. By contrast, a modular view of mind represents humans as much more like other animals. With this approach, humans too are seen as innately predisposed to understand the world in certain specified ways. Furthermore, there is nothing that goes against the assumption that they may well share some of these innate predispositions with other mammals. For example, the naïve physics of human infants probably closely resemble the naïve physics of other animals.

That of course is not to say that other predispositions may not be uniquely human. It is the general fact of having predispositions that links us to other animals. The specific human modules seem to be mainly connected to adaptations facilitating living in the type of society that characterises humans. Human social organisation is quite different from what is found in other animal species. Indeed, it is most probable that the ability to cope with the unique type of society in which we live would have had an important effect on our selective fitness in the distant past and would therefore have been positively selected and thus genetically inscribed in our mind. The language module itself is an obvious example of such an adaptation since it is partly language that makes our complex societies possible.

Another distinctive and unique human capacity is the ability to understand other minds. This too is also most probably the product of natural selection favouring the type of brain that it makes possible to live in human-type societies. The ability to read other minds implies something that has been called 'theory of mind' or 'naïve psychology'. In order to be able to read the minds of others we need a complex sub-conscious theory of what minds are like. Like language or face recognition this is something that it is unlikely could be simply learnt from experience. This is because it involves the largely necessarily sub-conscious supposition on our part that others are acting in terms of beliefs and desires. We behave towards the other in terms of our understanding of what we guess are their beliefs and desires rather than directly in terms of what they appear to be like externally. The complexity of human social life is thus built on this continual imagination of the minds of others. This is a process of ever increasing complexity since we act towards others not only in terms of what we believe others believe and desire but inevitably also in terms of what we believe others believe are our beliefs and desires, a process which can go on and on, at ever more levels. In other words, the most basic predisposition for social relations depends on genetically inherited capacities and not on ones which we could learn.

Such a modular perspective on the mind places human beings into a credible evolutionary context from which the anthropological theories of 'culture' had removed them. The return of humans into an evolutionary framework means that, as anthropologists, whenever we are trying to understand human behaviour we have, at the very least, to verify that our account is potentially compatible with what we know about the processes of the human mind evolved from only partially different types of ancestral minds.

The nature/culture wars

The effect of the modular revolution on anthropology is potentially enormous and in the next chapter it will be considered how it can make us revise some very classic anthropological work. However, until recently, nearly all social and cultural anthropologists have ignored its implications. This is probably in part because the most familiar application of modular theory to anthropological material has been to introduce the notion of 'culture free' elements existing within human cognition. Thus, the stress on 'universals' in the book by Pinker, discussed above, is given by him as a necessary consequence of modularity theory and which he argues is backed by the experimental work that seems to support it. It is therefore a short step to assume that these innate mechanisms for the understandings of the world that the modularists stress sufficiently account for elements of cognition and culture that are untouched by the maelstrom of communication which characterises the historical process. This kind of idea quickly leads to the labelling of certain features of human cognition as being 'cultural' while others are labelled 'natural' thus re-plunging us in the old and unhelpful opposition. This, however, rests on a misunderstanding. What modular theory proposes are predispositions which enter into the continual process of historical creation. It does not suggest the existence of elements which could remain outside this process.

The dangers of these misunderstandings become particularly clear when we look at some of the very strange projects it has encouraged. Thus, the neuro-psychologist Mark Hauser has carried out a very large-scale study intended to identify universal aspects of human morality and to demonstrate their consequent 'naturalness' (Hauser 2006). However, Hauser is faced with a familiar problem; he knows perfectly well that human moral codes, values and forms of reasoning vary from place to place. Thus, not carrying out female circumcision on girls is immoral for some Sudanese women, while for middle-class New Yorkers, it is immoral to do so. So Hauser decides to ignore variable cultural norms by defining them as 'merely cultural'. Then, in order to discover 'fundamental', 'natural' and 'universal' moral norms, he has tested the response of people from around the world to see how they would solve a hypothetical 'moral' problem. Since he wants to avoid the cultural he asks his informants for their response to a famous 'moral' conundrum, the so-called trolley problem, which corresponds to nothing anyone would ever encounter in real life. The subject is asked whether, within the context of a little scenario about trolleys on alternative tracks, it is right to actively kill a few people in order to save many. Hauser predicts, apparently rightly, that most people will say, after a bit of hesitation, that in certain cases that this is the right thing to do. In the Hauser experiment, the subjects are not given a chance to ask more questions, for example questions regarding the identity of the people concerned, nor are they furnished with more details about how such an odd situation has come about. In fact, if one asks people in different cultures what their solution to the trolley problem is they do seem to give similar answers. Their reaction to having to solve the problem is, however, quite different. The American university students who are the usual subjects of such experimentation see the problem as a puzzle, rather like a cross-word puzzle and quite enjoy doing so. What they do not display, however, is emotional tension or heart searching. They are used to these sorts of games and that is what the experiment is about for them. When I ask Malagasy villagers to solve the problem their reaction is of another kind. First of all, they want to know who the people concerned are, whether they are related to them, how old they are. In his experiment, Hauser would just not be able to take such factors into account. This would be so not only because of the way the experiment was set up but because he would feel that by doing so he would then be plunging into what he had decided to exclude in the first place, what he would call the 'cultural'.

Such problems show well the arbitrariness of trying to sort the cultural from the natural and the universal from the specific as though they were distinct. Even if the answers from the Malagasy villagers and the American students had been the same it is not at all clear what that would imply since the questions mean something quite different for either group. Furthermore, it is very doubtful that the answer would tell us anything about morality in the normal sense of the word. What the Malagasy villagers mean when they refuse to answer the question until they have more information is that the moral problem *only exists* when it is placed in a real lived context. In other words, that the division between the culturally variable and the universal which was implicit in the methodological set-up of the experiment is irrelevant to life as it is lived, which, after all, is what anthropologists and psychologists are attempting to study.

The motivation for a study such as that of Hauser, as well as for the arguments of Pinker, is the belief that the discovery of extensive modularity in humans should encourage the scholar to detect separate 'natural' and 'cultural' features. These then would have to be sorted out like sheep from goats but what the experiments show is that no such division can be meaningfully identified because it does not exist.

The misleading enterprise of looking for 'natural' bits and 'cultural' bits that the modular approach has sometimes produced is also found in the work of some Boasian cultural anthropologists. There too it produces equally misleading results. As we saw, Margaret Mead in her early book *Sex and Temperament in Three Primitive Societies* (1935) stresses the 'cultural' character of gender roles against what she considered the falsely naturalist interpretation of gender that she guesses the unenlightened American public would endorse. Following the logic of the binary nature of the nature/culture opposition, she assumes that if gender is not 'natural' it must be 'cultural'. However, with time, she began to have doubts about the pure cultural character of all aspects of gender. As a result, she produced a later work entitled *Male and Female* (1949) that concludes, equally misleadingly, that certain common attributes of women, and especially of men, are not cultural, and, following the old logic, she reasons that they then must be 'natural'. The result of this revision produces an arbitrary list of characters which are attributed to one side or the other of the nature/culture dichotomy. This division has not convinced many anthropologists who have rightly pointed out that there is nothing universal and therefore 'natural', as she seems to suggest, about the fact that women in Europe usually wear their hair long while men wear theirs short. This critique of a critique is, of course, equally caught in the old misleading dichotomy.

The attempt to separate 'cultural' and 'natural' features of gender roles has continued to obscure the subject as an endless string of different feminist authors have repeatedly accused each other of having considered this or that aspect as 'natural' when they should have considered it as 'cultural' (Rosaldo and Lamphere 1974; Ortner and Whitehead 1981; Collier and Yanagisako 1987; but see Laqueur 1990 for someone who avoids the trap).

A dynamic synthesis

Fortunately, the effects on anthropology of the modular revolution have not all been to push the subject back into the unhelpful framework of the old nature *versus* culture controversies. The root of the problem caused by the dichotomy has been its fundamentally static character while we are dealing with complex dynamics. Thus, implied by the concept of nature is a unified combination of processes: the processes of natural selection, the developmental process of birth and maturation, the ecological process of the life of particular species occurring amongst the dynamic of other living things, other individuals and even the non-living world. Similarly, implied by the concept of culture is the process of history. It is the unity and co-occurrence of all these processes that we as social or natural scientists should make the object of study.

The structuralism of Lévi-Strauss was an attempt to combine an understanding of the human brain with the unpredictable specificity of history. Lévi-Strauss is therefore a pioneer of the attempt at combining processes. The enterprise was abandoned by Lévi-Strauss himself who, as a result, never took into account the revolutionary implications of the modular revolution which fundamentally revised our understanding of the mind away from the *tabula rasa* that is implied in his theory.

Someone who has attempted to pick up the challenge where Lévi-Strauss abandoned it and to take into account the subsequent developments in cognitive science is Dan Sperber (1996). Sperber is well acquainted with both anthropology and cognitive science. He has been an enthusiastic advocate of the modular approach and has been influential in its development, but, unlike other modularists such as Pinker and Hauser, he does not see the modules directly producing 'universal natural bits'. As an anthropologist, Sperber accepts the Boasian point that all elements of culture are unique and he recognises that it is misleading to pretend that what makes every case different is only a matter of superficial frills. He too stresses the complexity of the immense disorderly and infinitely intricate 'conversation' that is human culture taken as a whole since its unclear beginnings more than 150,000 years ago. He therefore eschews any idea of a unilineal or predictable trajectory for human history and the accompanying search for pristine universals within the ethnographic record. In his perspective, human beings are continually recreating what they have learnt from others and modifying it. He also emphasises that the meme-type idea which implies that we just receive information, store it and pass it on untouched is a misrepresentation of the much more tentative process through which we imagine what others intend to mean and then, as best we can, sometimes attempt to recreate it in an inevitably somewhat different form (Sperber 2001). Such an uncertain process is what creates differentiation at both the individual and the social level. In all that he is a good Boasian. What makes him different, however, is that for him the general modular dispositions of the human mind are significant and create a degree of regularity in that they influence the differential likelihood that certain representations become common or are lost. Because of the existence of modules, certain representations are more congenial and therefore more likely to be stored in individual brains and therefore, also, to be reproduced with greater accuracy. Such responsive representations are particularly 'catchy' and they therefore spread easily within a population. But the fact that the mental modules favour certain cultural content over other possible content is in no way a sufficient explanation of its occurrence or its character. Modular preferences are only one factor, among many, that explain the presence of certain beliefs or ideas in a particular place at a particular time. They are also not sufficient explanations of the frequency of such beliefs and ideas within a population. For example, Sperber argues that it would be ridiculous to explain the spread of the technology of the internal combustion engine, simply in terms of the fact that it is easily thinkable and memorable, without *also* taking into account the probably much more important factor that such engines clearly work well. By contrast, witchcraft-like ideas that are probably of no practical value and that mistakenly explain misfortune in terms of the secret ill will of others, spread easily in a population and thus become part of its culture simply because natural selection has developed in humans a brain with a modular innate vigilance and even suspicion towards others. This comes to mean that we are always overzealously on the look out for hidden malevolence because this is necessary in the peculiarly complex type of society within which, as a result of evolution, humans live. According to such an argument, the modular predisposition is not for witchcraft in the specific cultural form found in any particular culture; it is less specific than that, but it will mean that a specific and unique concept of witchcraft, if it arises in a particular time and place, has a good chance of sparking an epidemic of accusations. On the other hand, the demonstration that witchcraft-like beliefs are nonsense will only become established and remain in a population if this argument is continually repeated through the continuous effort of regular demonstration in institutions such as schools or churches.

Overall, such an approach is clearly in accord with the point that the diffusionists made against the evolutionist: that the potential of the human brain means that human history is a quite different phenomenon to the history activated by natural selection. However, for all that, it does not run into the problem created by the drift of the diffusionists towards cultural relativism and anti-naturalism, the idea that cultures are not, in any way, bound by the nature of the human body and brain, a position made totally unlikely by the kind of findings on which the modularists rely. The problem is simply that even though the early evolutionists misleadingly exaggerated cultural recurrences, as for example of the kind of phenomena that they called 'totemism', the denial that any recurrent element exists is probably even more problematic since it ignores the obvious regularities found in unconnected places. These regularities anthropologists are forced, however unwillingly, to recognise again and again (Lévi-Strauss 1962). Sperber explains these by the recurrent elements caused by the mind's predispositions for certain contents, but he does so without denying the fundamental uniqueness of each case, the point that is rightly so important for social and cultural anthropologists. This is because the mental processes only exist in conjunction with other processes.

One could thus paraphrase the Sperber thesis as saying that the modular mind is a product of natural selection, and thus is as it is as a result of the rationale of evolution, while culture is the product of a totally different process created in part by individuals in ways that, so far at least, we cannot account for in general terms. The two systems interact because the mind *selects* representations in terms of their differential accord, or otherwise, with our modular predispositions. The Sperber thesis is thus a great advance on the misleading sorting out of items of knowledge into a universal (natural) box and a variable (cultural) box which suggests that there are elements untouched by the historical process or by the species-wide natural process. It brings together history and natural history while not collapsing the one or the other. This relative independence may well be simply the inevitable result of the fact that the two are working on such different time scales. At least it would be very difficult to study their connection since the relevant evolutionary time for the emergence of a distinctly human brain probably involves at least several million years while the relevant period of human history is probably not more than 200,000 years. As a result, the period of co-occurrence is very short on an evolutionary time scale.

There is, however, a serious limitation to the Sperber approach, at least as it was originally formulated. Within it, the psychological process of selection and the historical process remain quite separate and so there is no room for understanding how they modify each other as they come together in the life of the individual. The model is mechanical, more like two cogs interacting in a watch rather than biological and transformative. For example, it cannot focus on, or try to explain, the transformations in the content of representations as they are used in the process of life, nor the inflections and transformations of the modular mind as it is modified by the representations it is continually encountering and absorbing. In order for that complex and dynamic interaction to be fully understood, yet another process must be taken into account.

This other process[1] involves a consideration of the modifications of the implications of the modular predispositions which occur during maturation and indeed throughout the life of individuals. This had not been much considered by the original modularists, largely because the presence of modular predispositions had been demonstrated almost exclusively in experimental work on young infants.

The original clash between Chomsky and Piaget was over the *tabula rasa* issue, and on the whole Chomsky won. However, this apparent victory led modularists to forget for a time the greatest contribution of Piaget's work: the focus on the importance of continual development of what cognitive psychologists were studying. Chomskian theories and

---

[1] Yet further processes are relevant but cannot be discussed here. One of the most important ones is the effect of the environment, both internal and external, which is also being transformed by the very presence of humans.

subsequent arguments for a modular view of the mind were at first presented as leading to an irresoluble clash with older Piagetian views of cognitive development. More recently, however, a number of theoreticians have argued for a synthesis of both approaches, one that would take valuable elements from both. A number of psychologists who focus on child development have thus pointed to one misleading implication of the way modularity theory was represented by some of its early proponents. These had seemed to suggest that a normal infant possesses innately fixed chunks of information that are not subsequently modified by the process of development. This is how Pinker and Hauser seem to think of modular knowledge. Such a static view of the knowledge of the individual was in conflict with what Piaget had demonstrated and stressed again and again. This was the fact that cognitive development is a process of continual and radical transformations. Thus, the developmental perspective of the new modularists inevitably changes the focus from the attempt to identify the semantic content of a module as fixed, once and for all, to a consideration of the modular mind within the framework of the continuous cognitive change that happens with maturation as the child grows up and as the adult learns ever more. This approach has encouraged a great deal of highly innovative experimental work that has, in turn, led to fundamental theoretical changes. Thus, Carey and Spelke are able to represent individual cognitive change as a succession of 'revolutions' comparable to the scientific revolutions of Kuhn's interpretation of the history of science (Carey and Spelke 1994) during which the original modular content is considerably modified during development. The mind is envisaged not just as a receptor of information, as in the meme model, but as a transformer of information, as in the Sperber model. This, however, is taken further since the transformation is partly on the basis of previous knowledge and of maturation. In a somewhat analogous way Karmiloff-Smith talks of a process which she calls 'representational rediscription' whereby the child revises and re-represents her knowledge (Karmiloff-Smith 1999) as she grows up making what she has learnt previously the subject of further reflection revised in the light of exposition to new situations and new ideas.

The developmental approach profoundly modifies the way we understand the relation of the modular theory of mind and culture. From this perspective, modules and their semantic potential are not anymore seen as causing the presence of pre-cultural or natural knowledge but instead they are understood as learning devices which are themselves modified by what is learnt. As in Sperber's perspective, they enable us to learn preferentially certain types of contents from others but this does not mean that the processes leave matters as they were with the selective effect of modules on representations just re-occurring, itself unmodified, as if from zero, whenever new knowledge is encountered. Rather, as in the Piagetian model, the effect of assimilation of knowledge by the child creates a new state of affairs. It profoundly modifies the cognitive mechanisms and the way new representations are dealt with. The cognitive development of the child is itself also in a fundamental process of transformation.

When discussing Lévi-Strauss and Piaget in the earlier part of this chapter, I pointed out how the two are close in some respect but with opposite blind spots. Lévi-Strauss focuses on the individual brain as it is plunged into history. This is also true in Sperber's model but there the individual brain is understood as much more complex because modularity is taken into account. Lévi-Strauss and Sperber, by combining an understanding of the brain and an understanding of the great conversation, thus bring evolution and historical processes together. However, the missing element in Lévi-Strauss's and also in Sperber's theoretical synthesis is their lack of consideration of the individual cognitive developmental process. Piaget, on the other hand, makes this central but forgets about the placing of the individual within the historical process of the great conversation. However, if we think of human cognitive life as the merging of all these processes which Lévi-Strauss, Sperber and Piaget put together and add to this the developmental perspective of such as that of Spelke, Carey and Karmiloff-Smith, we can begin at last to grasp the full complexity of human cognition in history. We are dealing with a single process but it is one which at least has the different dynamics inseparably unified. With such a perspective, we realise that all the various attempts at opposing 'nature' and 'culture' were simply attempts at not having to face the difficulties of the full complication of human cognition, a complication which results from the unique character of our species. What anthropologists, psychologists and other cognitive scientists are dealing with is a mind, for which evolution has made the historical process part of the natural. This unified natural phenomenon is these disciplines' only and common subject matter.

The methodological implications of the unity of 'nature' and 'culture'

Perhaps overcoming what the rhetorical dichotomy 'nature and culture' had misleadingly created is not all that difficult if we think of human cognition not as a state but as a single process, the dynamics of which can be temporally heuristically distinguished as history and individual cognitive developmental transformation occurring *together*. However, the methodological implications of such a conclusion are fundamental and are much more difficult to overcome. These are at the root of some repeated misunderstandings that occur when social/cultural anthropologists and natural scientists try to co-operate.

One can put the matter over simply by saying that the theoretical starting point of, for example, a cognitive psychologist is 'external' while the starting point of a social anthropologist is 'internal'. The analytical tools of the psychologist, the questions she asks, the categories of analysis she uses – categories such as 'concepts' or 'mind' – have all been defined in a discourse that is external to the subjects of the enquiry. On the other hand, anthropologists try to use the cognitive tools of the person, or persons, they study as a foundation on which to base their analysis. These tools are inevitably only related and moulded to the particular place and the particular time where that subject is located. The significance of using this 'internal' baseline has been stressed by anthropologists again and again, perhaps most eloquently by Malinowski with his well-known phrase 'from the native's point of view'.

With such different starting points, putting the two types of work together might appear as quixotic as grafting a human arm onto a cloud. However, although the metaphor may reflect the defeatism that often comes from both sides, it greatly exaggerates the difficulty.

This is, first of all, because the gulf between the 'native's' point of view and that of the natural scientist is nowhere as great as much anthropology and cognitive science has pretended it is. Such a stance made anthropology forget, when, in the heat of controversy it has wanted to declare itself 'cultural' and not 'natural', that both the scientist and the people studied live in roughly the same world which is governed by the same laws of physics, biology, chemistry and social organisation and that both have similar brains moulded by evolution in order to deal with this same physical, biological, chemical and social world. There is thus a sense in which both points of view are 'internal' but not internal to any particular group or individual but internal to the human species as a whole. The misleading illusion of absolute distance between scientist and ethnographer is the product of the historically created opposition between 'nature' and 'culture' which produces the anthropological fantasy of a super exotic 'culture' that could exist outside 'nature'. My first conclusion is, therefore, that anthropologists have, in reality, no choice but to be 'externalist' (that is human internalist) when they think they are being internalist from the point of view of a particular group. This is so for a number of reasons, some of which have as much to do with the non-human world as with the characteristics of the mind.

The other fact which explains why the gulf is not as great as it might at first seem is that the idea of a totally external stance, which the cognitive scientist may believe she is adopting, is impossible. (I am not here talking of the much-debated issue of the degree of cultural construction of science.) The reason is that the joint aim of all cognitive scientists, anthropologists as much as the other members of that coalition, is to understand the behaviour of actual humans as they exist in the world which they inhabit. This world only exists for them within the process of history as this is the distinctive characteristic of our species. As a result, even allowing for the powerful constraints put on it by the general human evolved brain, it is not identical for all or any people. For example, the nature of the contact between a mother and her child an hour after it is born is not identical in Edinburgh, a Japanese city or a Malagasy village. This is, in large part, explained by the differences in behaviour of people in different places and times as well as by the differences in the material and institutional environment within which people live.

Furthermore, the specificities which human history creates should not be thought of as merely creating an environment for people but also, to a certain but significant extent, creating the very people who live within that environment. This is most obvious in the cognitive field but in fact it also applies to all aspects of ourselves even to the shape of our bones. There are no non-cultural bits of us as there are no non-natural bits. We are made by a single but complex process that creates, *inter alia*, specificity. Differentiation produced by history is one of the specific aspects of our species, rather like the shape of our femur. Ignoring this crucial aspect of what it is to be a member of our species is as daft as studying human locomotion while pretending that we have femurs like those of baboons.

The fact of the continual process of historical construction of human beings has the methodological implication that if we want to explain human action, rather than merely describe it, we have no alternative but to remember that it is brought about by people from the inside. It is from the 'inside' that people live their lives, though that does not mean that this inside is free of the implications of the neurological mechanisms of our brain or of the nature of the world (though we should remember that both the brain and the world are, to a certain extent, themselves continually changing). The reality is therefore that a psychologist studying cognition, like an anthropologist, has no alternative but to take also an 'internal' inflected point of view if they want to study such things as human cognitive development, or irony. The psychological literature on such topics shows that this is in fact what is done. Similarly, the anthropologist cannot for an instant imagine that this 'inside' is free floating.

The reason why co-operation between scholars such as anthropologists and cognitive scientists is in fact much easier than it might seem is because neither side is quite what they believe they are. The externalism of natural science, as it applies to human cognition, is much more internalist than it often makes out. The internalism of interpretative anthropology is much more externalist than it sometimes imagines. What has often obscured this is the futility of the nature/culture dichotomy. The fact that the disciplines are closer than they believe they are does not, however, completely eliminate the epistemological problem but it greatly diminishes it.

And the ultimate reason why interpretative anthropologists and cognitive scientists are closer than they believe is not far to seek. The difficulty in working together is often attributed to the chasm between nature and culture, to different intellectual traditions or even to different criteria of truth, but it is above all due to the complex nature of the animal we are. It is because humans are within a single process where different types of driving forces produce a unified movement. It is very very difficult for anthropologists and others to study our species, whatever the academic department we are affiliated to, but this is less because of epistemological incompatibilities and more because of the complex nature of the phenomena we are dealing with.

However, we have to recognise that if recent development in cognitive science theory offers ways that seem to invite fruitful collaboration, the desirability of such reunion is not obvious to most social and cultural

anthropologists. This is because the final outcome of the diffusionists'
stress on the particularity of every case has been to transform anthropology away from the generalising science that, in the work of the early
evolutionists, it had prematurely pretended to be, and changing it into
the total opposite, an anti-naturalist study of an infinity of ethnographic
cases. Ethnography, in the mind of many anthropologists, does not need
to concern itself with general questions. After all, why should a study of
a Malaysian factory need concern itself with any general questions about
the working of the mind? The following chapter is devoted to showing that even with such reduced ambitions, the ethnographer ignores the
general discussions about the nature of human cognition that this chapter
has discussed at her peril. It will also show how challenging ethnography
in this way actually enables us to move the joint programme of cognitive
and social scientists forward.

FIVE

Time and the anthropologists

The basic argument of the previous chapters was that the reason why anthropologists cannot ignore the work of cognitive scientists, and for that matter vice versa, was that what they study is a phenomenon that is both cognitive and historical. If we attempt to separate the two, as the opposition between 'nature' and 'culture' attempts to do, we are left without a subject matter. The attempt on the part of anthropologists to ignore the cognitive simply leads them to making assumptions in their writing which, because they are merely implicit, are not critically examined. The purpose of this chapter is twofold. First, it shows the presence of these unexamined and therefore dangerous cognitive assumptions in texts which make no reference to empirical or theoretical work in psychology. Secondly, it will show how, if we scrutinise the implicit psychological assumptions present in the anthropological work and place these side by side with what we know from cognitive science, we can not only question some of the propositions that have been made as they stand, but also reveal hidden riches in the anthropological accounts that enable us to formulate questions for future research in both anthropology and cognitive psychology. This chapter is thus a demonstration of the value of studying people in society as a single historical and psychological process.

Such an exercise has also another purpose. Even though I argued in the conclusion of the previous chapter that the work of the cognitive scientist and the interpretative anthropologist was closer than both sides imagine, the reader of the book might well ask how one can go one step further and suggest how the two disciplines can co-operate in practice in what they each have to say about cognition. Here, I focus on the particularly important issue of time and I propose how co-operation between cognitive and social sciences can move forward our understanding of issues central to both types of disciplines in a way that cannot occur when they work separately. This does not, at first at least, require new types of research by either psychologists or anthropologists but a critical re-examination of findings already obtained. By criticising the achievements of the different disciplinary specialists in the light of knowledge that comes from the other we can, simply by this means, move things forward.

Anthropological ethnographies of time

This chapter consists principally of an examination of two famous studies by anthropologists and especially of what they have to say about the cognition of time. These are the books *The Nuer* by E. E. Evans-Pritchard (1940) and *The Fame of Gawa* by Nancy Munn (1986). Before considering these two works in detail, however, it is necessary to be reminded of the history of the way the topic of the cognition of time has been created in the social sciences. This will put in context the theoretical stance of the authors.

As we saw in the previous chapters, one of the most nefarious effects of imagining the social sciences, and most particularly anthropology, as a kind of liberator from the imprisoning power of modern science and enlightenment rationality has been to obscure the very contributions which these disciplines might make to a general and balanced understanding of human beings. It has made the combination of subjects such as evolutionary biology and cultural anthropology almost impossible because it plunges such attempts in shadowy and menacing controversies of uncertain nature.

The topic of the cognition of time illustrates well how anthropologists' fear of such disciplines as cognitive psychology has led them to say very strange things and has hindered them in more soberly evaluating their own contributions.

When writing about time, social scientists often see their role as that of defending humans against an insufficiently 'cultural' representation, which they impute to 'natural' scientists. According to this story, biologists or psychologists naïvely believe humans take in temporal information merely as unthinking cameras photographing the unmediated facts and organise their actions in response to innate animal clocks. Social scientists such as anthropologists, by contrast, comfortable in what they consider is their greater sophistication, point to the historically constructed 'cultural' evaluations of time and how these relate to different social, political, economic, philosophical and aesthetic factors.

Furthermore, social scientists have, at least since the beginning of the twentieth century, felt that showing a social or a cultural influence on our perception and conceptualisation of time would be one of their sweetest and juiciest victories over natural scientists and philosophers. The reason is quite obvious: a certain conceptualisation of time underlies all arguments in the natural sciences and classical philosophy. Thus, Newtonian physics involves a view of time as an abstract, uniform and measurable dimension, and, although modern physics has since dramatically changed the specialist's understanding, this has hardly had an influence on ordinary, day to day, thinking or, for that matter, on most science. Thus, if the concept of time was shown to be the product of culture, the natural sciences would become mere sub-disciplines of anthropology. In this way, once again, the debate is set within the framework of all the old misleading dichotomies, especially that of nature *versus* culture.

But the issue is not just scientific; it is also obscurely political. The history of the European politics of time goes right back to the fact that enlightenment writers, such as Voltaire, for example, felt that, because Newtonian physics seemed to rest on a universal and natural authority, it would be one of the best tools with which to fight the obscurantism of the established orders of the church and of royal absolutism which, they argued, rested on arbitrary and limited concepts. The attraction to the scientific laws of nature was for these thinkers an appeal to an even higher authority which outflanked the legitimacy of those who sought to control their subjects and their laity. As a result, particularly in France, the faith in science was linked to the overthrow of the *Ancien Régime* and ultimately the rationalism of science became associated with certain forms of modern universalist liberal political theory. Subsequently, however, things changed and by the late nineteenth century and during the first half of the twentieth century a reaction in intellectual circles set in. Discomfort with the liberal enlightenment's political stance emerged for a number of different reasons. Such criticisms were often linked to various forms of reactionary conservatism but also to a number of new radical ideologies. This strange dual parentage led to various criticisms of universalist rationalist thinking from the point of view of 'culture'. This type of argument influenced, and was influenced by, anthropology, most famously in the work of Durkheim and his followers. More recently, after the events of 1968 in France, another, apparently new, libertarian reaction against enlightenment thinking set in. This included a very belated reaction against the theories of the late nineteenth-century anthropologists which were discussed in chapter 3. The focus of the reaction was above all against the old alliance of natural science and the Voltairean liberal tradition, although the proximate focus of attack was Marxism since this was seen as one of its avatars. In a variety of ways, this led to the revival of the old Boasian criticism of the evolutionists because certain forms of Marxism had incorporated these anthropological theories, especially those of Morgan. Also included in the line of fire were the theories of Lévi-Strauss because they were seen as too naturalist and they were thus lumped together with explicit and implicit evolutionary theories. As the target of these new 'culturalists' were, *inter alia*, the anthropological evolutionists, it seemed to follow that the old opponents of these theories were the allies of the opponents of the scientific pretentions of grand theories such as Marxism; this on the well-known principle that the enemies of our enemies are our friends. Thus, the intellectual heroes of the post-1968 movement, such as Foucault, Derrida and a number of others, embraced, usually with somewhat ill-informed enthusiasm, post-Boasian anthropology in their search for confirmation of such propositions as the 'cultural' variability of such fundamental concepts as time, persons and truth. For their part, anthropologists, especially North American ones, welcomed these writers since they seemed to confirm, from the outside, what their discipline had more timidly been claiming for somewhat different reasons since the beginning of the century. Such debates and alliances have subsequently had reverberations well beyond the social sciences, in some cases quite unexpected ones. Thus, the message that the 'others' have different systems of time turns up in a very influential book by David Landes, *The Wealth and Poverty of Nations*, where he explains the superiority of Europe in part by 'the Judeo-Christian sense of linear time, while other societies thought of time as cyclical' (Landes 1998: p. 59).

This background shows how wide ranging are the implications of the controversy over the cognition of time. In order to focus this discussion, I first turn to the earlier anthropological writers whose work lies at the back of these controversies and who were to lay the theoretical foundations of many modern anthropological claims about temporality. In particular, I shall consider the theories of the American Whorf and the French Durkheim in whose work we see the attraction for anti-liberal conservatives of libertarian stances whose claims seem to relativise the hard sciences for the greater glory of such disciplines as anthropology and sociology, often with arguments about the basis of the cognition of time.

The American anthropological anti-universalist tradition found its most explicit formulation in the work of Benjamin Lee Whorf. Whorf was a pupil of Sapir who in turn was a pupil of Boas. Boas's intellectual roots have been much discussed recently; as we saw in the previous chapter his anti-evolutionism was partly motivated by the political situation in the United States at the time when he was writing and, before that, by the German romantic backlash against the enlightenment perceived as French, at least in Germany. This had led to a stress on the equal valorisation of different cultures against universalist scientific claims. In the work of Whorf, this type of opposition to science becomes the basis of a characteristically American alliance with Christian Fundamentalism (see Carroll's introduction to Whorf 1964).

Whorf argued for a homology between habitual thought, culture and language (1941). He argued that different languages represented duration in different ways and that, therefore, people who spoke different types of languages apprehended time differently, thus: 'concepts of "time" and "matter" are not given in substantially the same form by experience to all men, but depend upon the nature of language, or languages, through the use of which they have been developed' (Whorf (1941) 1964: p. 158). In a significant and typical way, Whorf uses this insight to relativise Newtonian physics. According to him, the latter is dependent on our 'intuition', but this is no true intuition, it is not 'natural'; it is the product of 'culture' since it is the product of 'the recepts from culture and language. That is where Newton got them' (1964: p. 153). The differentiation between language communities and their accompanying conceptual systems had come about, Whorf explains, through history. According to him, we find the source of Newton's ideas when we go back to the history of the Hebrew language and to the subsequent history of Greek and Latin. For the origin of Hopi language and thought, however (the Hopi being Whorf's prototypical other), we would similarly have to go to their formative linguistic and cultural past, but unfortunately this is impossible because it is lost and so we cannot 'read' it (1964: p. 157).

But, in fact, Whorf's evidence for the effect of language on thought, especially as it relates to the issue of time, was weak in the extreme. Although it was the keystone of his argument, most recent work has denied such strong determinist connection between the type of tenses and moods of the verbs of a particular language and the thought processes of its speakers. Those who have recently attempted to rescue Whorf's arguments have pointed to effects of language on thought that fall far far short of Whorf's grandiose claims (Slobin 1991; Lucy 1992; Boroditsky 2001; Levinson 2003).[1]

In Europe, it was Emile Durkheim and his pupils of the French sociological school, usually referred to by the name of its journal, the *Année sociologique*, who approached the subject of time frontally. Durkheim's politics ultimately became dominated by his attempt to reassert a traditionalist moralism which he believed, like other types of conservatives, had been dangerously damaged by the various French revolutions. However, he differed from these other French conservatives in seeking to legitimate this traditional morality by non-monarchist and non-Catholic means.

Durkheim had started his career as a relatively orthodox philosopher, much influenced by Kant. Kant had argued that the Aristotelian categories of understanding, of which time is the foremost, had to be taken for granted and to be beyond conscious questioning before any less fundamental forms of understanding was possible. For him, these categories are the 'framework' or the 'bone structure' of knowledge. Nothing in human individual experience can be the source of our cognition of time since, without its *a priori* framework, an individual cannot make sense of the world nor can knowledge be shared between different people since they do not have the same parameters. This position was Durkheim's starting point; however, he disagreed with Kant as to a necessarily supernatural character for the origin of a category such as time. For Durkheim, it was society that was the source of our categories, though society created them through an indirect process involving ritual which, rather

---

[1] There are still some who would maintain Whorf's claim but in very watered down form, e.g. Lucy 1992, but see also Malotki 1983.

mysteriously, ensured their categorical nature. This was because ritual created the necessary *illusion* that the categories were not man made but come from external sources (Durkheim 1912; 1960).

It is interesting to note the kind of ethnographic data Durkheim used for discovering the categorical understanding of time in a given population. This is significant since many anthropologists, following in his footsteps, have mistakenly seen the matter in similar terms. For him, the categorical cognition of time is very largely equated with the conventional divisions we use to measure it. For example, in the European tradition these are units such as minutes, days and seasons. Durkheim seems to believe that these divisions are what create our framework for knowing time.

One of the effects of the difference between Kant and Durkheim in what they saw as the source of understandings of time was that Kant implied that all humans perceived time identically. This was because the categories had a single transcendental source external to anything going on in any particular place on earth. By contrast, Durkheim explicitly argued that people understood time differentially since for him the type of society was the source of time cognition. It follows that since there were different types of societies, time is understood in varied ways in varied types of societies. He finds confirmation of this in the obvious fact that different people use different measures of time. Thus he is able to criticise Kant's transcendentalism by saying that 'the categories of understanding are never fixed; they change according to place and time' (1912; 1960: p. 21). Finally, and typically of many anthropologists since, Durkheim finally turns to a discussion of the nature of science (1912; 1960: pp. 616 and 635 and indeed throughout his conclusion) which, he argues, depends on shared categories of understanding which for him are religious in origin since religion and society are equivalent.

As a result, Durkheim, who at first seems as different as it is possible to be from the American cultural anthropologists, is ultimately very close to Whorf on this particular matter, and, although he does not attribute such a key role to the type of language spoken by people, even this element is not totally absent from his thought (1912; 1960: p. 620). Both authors claim that, at its most fundamental, our cognition of time varies as a result of the type of knowledge which has been passed on to us through history by the members of our society and both argue that this particular, ultimately arbitrary, knowledge falsely seems to normal people to be beyond question and to be 'natural'. In this fundamental matter, both implicitly rule out, first, the possibility that it is something about the external non-human world, as it is and as it is lived, which requires certain types of time tools and, secondly, the possibility that it is something about our biological nature, which of course includes our mental nature, which determines our temporal understanding. Significantly, both use evidence of cultural variation as a kind of proof of the irrelevance of these two possibilities.

The point of going over these older theories in anthropology is not simply to show their convergences but because these theories have continually recurred in subsequent anthropological writing and have recently been again welcomed by a certain intellectual public for, I suspect, the very same political reason that appealed when they were first formulated. It is no accident that 'science studies' are at the moment such a popular thing to do in American anthropology departments. The main point seems again to be to show the social origin of the tools scientists take as categorical (Latour and Woolgar 1979).[2] Similarly, these are also the reasons why certain philosophisers who make all, or some, of the same points have struck such a chord with contemporary social scientists. This unexpected coming together of theorists of such different types as Durkheim and Whorf on such a fundamental point as the cognition of time has meant that many anthropologists have been able to produce arguments which combine their points of view, without seeming aware of their

---

[2] Since the publication of this book Latour has radically changed his position but this seems to have had little effect on anthropologists (Latour 2005).

very different origins and implications. What follows in this chapter are actual examples of the kind of anthropological and ethnographic studies which shows how these ideas have been influential in the United States and Britain.

The Nuer

One of the most famous books of twentieth-century anthropology is surely Evans-Pritchard's study of the Nuer of the Sudan (Evans-Pritchard 1940). There can be no doubt that this reputation is justly deserved and the influence of this text has been enormous. One of the middle chapters of the book is devoted to the cognition of time and space, in Evans-Prichard's words, to the Nuer's 'concepts of time'. Although not mentioned by name, this chapter is clearly in harmony with Durkheim in that part of the argument is the proposition that Nuer thought about time is determined by their social organisation. The chapter parallels closely an essay by Durkheim's pupil Marcel Mauss about Eskimo concepts of time and space (Mauss 1906).

Evans-Pritchard identifies two types of factors as determining Nuer conceptualisation of time. The first is the social, which he calls 'structural'. The second he calls 'ecological'.[3] By ecological, Evans-Pritchard means the productive activity of the people, taking place in the particular constricting context of the natural environment in which the Nuer live. The Nuer inhabit an environment where, as a result of annual flooding of the rivers due to heavy rains, they have to migrate seasonally. This means that approximately half the year is spent in plain villages where the main activity is focussed on cattle keeping and the other half of the year, during periods when the rivers flood everywhere except the hills, the Nuer retreat to elevated camps where their main activity is agriculture.

---

[3] Evans-Pritchard uses the spelling oecological.

Paradoxically, this is when they are in closest contact with their animals. The annual rhythm of transhumance means that the productive activities and the physical and social environment are quite different at different times of the year and this contrast also dominates their lives and the way they talk about these different times of the year. As is so often the case, this division is further heightened by the fact that certain rituals occur at specific times of the year, that is in much the same way as Christmas was inevitably associated with the low point in the agricultural year for medieval peasants.

Social time: structural time, in Evans-Pritchard's terms, is linked to this contrast in demographic organisation during different times of the year. This is particularly significant for Nuer kinship organisation into lineages. From the point of view of the individual, lineages are rather like Russian dolls. Thus, for example, a person's immediate lineage – the descendants in the male line of a man's grandfather together with their wives – form an inner core to a larger lineage. This could consist of the descendants of the same man's great-great-great-grandfather. Such larger lineage will contain other small lineages, but it will also be, in turn, a part of a still larger lineage, and so on. Thus, the founding ancestors of small contained lineages are more recent ancestors than the founders of the larger inclusive lineages. This means that kinship closeness or distance has clear temporal implications, in much the same way that one could consider a sister as connected to oneself by a more recent link in time than a second cousin because the tie, in the one case, is caused by events occurring at the parental generation while, in the other, at the great-grandparental generation. Overall, Evans-Pritchard is thus able to argue that the Nuer concept of time comes from two sources: first, from their particular engagement with the world in a particular place, and, secondly, from the rules which, from their perspective, govern the formation of kinship groups, especially local and lineage groups.

Evans-Pritchard quite convincingly argues that these factors are of very great importance to the Nuer. They are not exactly 'culture' in the way a writer such as Boas would envisage it, in that they are not separate from practical activity. They are much more the kind of things Durkheim had in mind, but the argument does imply, *inter alia*, the simple basic proposition which both Whorf and Durkheim would have accepted: that time is not the same for the Nuer as it is for 'us' since we live in different environments, since we make our living in the world in different ways and since our societies are organised differently.

So, according to Evans-Pritchard, what effects do these ecological and structural factors have on the Nuer cognition of time? First of all, the divisions of the year provide 'the conceptual poles in time reckoning' (p. 96). Ecological time therefore 'appears to be, and is, cyclical' (p. 95). 'The calendar is a relation between a cycle of activities and a conceptual cycle and the two cannot fall apart since it is from the former that the latter derives its meaning and function' (pp. 95–100). Other cycles are also important to the Nuer. There is the cycle of the sun during the day, but this is dominated by the various tasks linked with cattle keeping, which Evans-Pritchard wittily says, constitute a 'cattle clock'. Then there are the cycles of the moon, but these latter matter much less to the Nuer and they do not attempt a mathematical adjustment between them and the yearly seasonal cycle.

These various points concerning the way the Nuer talk about the measurement of time lead Evans-Pritchard to a more general conclusion. The vagueness of their calculations and the practical and social emphasis mean that

Though I have spoken of time and units of time, the Nuer have no expression equivalent to 'time' in our language, and they cannot, therefore, as we can, speak of time as though it were something actual, which passes, can be wasted, can be saved, and so forth. I do not think that they ever experience the same feeling of fighting against time or having to co-ordinate activities with an abstract passage of time, because their points of reference are mainly the activities themselves, which are generally of a leisurely character. Events follow a logical order, but they are not controlled by an abstract system, there being no autonomous points of reference to which activities have to conform with precision. Nuer are fortunate. (p. 103)

The Nuer is thus a particularly clear and elegant early example of a type of argument which is recurrent in many ethnographies. It has proved very influential, but the same sort of writing can be found springing from a whole variety of origins. Before critically evaluating this particular manifestation of such a general anthropological tendency, it is, however, necessary to turn to a more recent but equally important work by an American anthropologist.

The Fame of Gawa

The central theoretical argument of the famous book by Nancy Munn, *The Fame of Gawa* (1986), involves showing how the process of ordinary living and action, here called 'practice', organises people's thoughts, language and actions. Munn argues that what she calls the 'construction' of space and time is central to this process of continual definition. She seeks, she tells us, the 'intersubjective' feeling of the actors; she is seeking the 'existential' form of understanding and emotion of the people of Gawa (p. 268). Though she tells us that she does not want to separate the cognitive from other aspects of life, she does not deny that this 'constructive' process involves, at the very least, the mental. In the introductory chapter to the book, significantly entitled 'The conceptual framework', she defines her theoretical position in the following way:

Thus it is not merely as Giddens (1981: p. 30) has put it, that 'time space relations are . . . constitutive features of social systems', but additionally that the 'situated practices', which in Giddens's terms make up these systems, themselves *construct* different formations of spacetime. As I have argued elsewhere (Munn 1983: p. 280), socio-cultural practices 'do not simply go on *in* or *through* time and space, but (they also) . . . constitute (create) the space

91

time…in which they "go on"' [all italics in the original].[4] (Munn 1986: pp. 10–11)

There is much to be said for this and I shall return to what may be meant in other parts of this book but, at least, at this stage, we may note two inevitable implications of such a formulation. First, it is that the 'conceptual framework', especially of time and space, must be very different in different places in the world where different forms of practice go on. This is necessary since, if practice creates cognition and practice in Gawa is different from practice in, for example, Austria, then conceptualisation in the two places must be very different. Secondly, even if we consider only one place, space and time conceptualisation are in a state of continual flux because, as people engage in the different types of practices that life involves, time becomes continually modified since we are told this applies to the conceptualisation of 'space time' and therefore of time itself.

The evidence for this intersubjective 'construction' through 'practice', on the little Atoll of Gawa, is what constitutes most of the book. However, what it discusses in most detail is the Kula ceremonial exchange system, famously described by Malinowski for the Trobriands, but which also takes place in Gawa. Munn follows Malinowski's insistence on contextualisation by linking the symbolism of the Kula to such things as witchcraft, ideas concerning the production and consumption of food, gender, mortuary practices and much else.[5] Through this type of writing, she succeeds very well in making us intuit how the people of Gawa understand and seek to achieve 'fame', especially through Kula exchanges and, more modestly, through hospitality. She explains how the desire for fame

---

[4] This statement is accompagnied by a footnote which does not seem to modify fundamentally the text.

[5] Rather bizarrely, she claims this linking of these different topics is an innovation while of course this type of thing was one of the main aims of the continually referred to *Argonauts of the Western Pacific*.

relates to the cognition of time. Thus, in passages such as the following she refers to the joking demands for reciprocity or hospitality at a future time that are made as a way of closing episodes of commensality: 'we can see clearly the sense in which an attempt is being made to transform intersubjective spacetime positively, as recipients in the process of acquiring kula shells or food are directed to project the current experience of receiving in terms of their future, reciprocal giving' (p. 65).

It is indeed clear what Munn is talking about. As the people of Gawa engage in various types of actions and as they talk they evoke different territories of space and time. Thus marriage alliances evoke the distances between the homes of spouses and the gifts which move along these 'paths'. As they negotiate and plan Kula exchanges, the people of Gawa evoke past moments when gifts were transferred and as they hope for and perhaps imagine future transactions. In a sense, therefore, evoked times and spaces are continually changing in a way that is both individual and social in that these evocations are often shared and organised by social and cultural activities.

I have no problem with Munn's argument phrased in this way and nothing but admiration for the skill with which she supports it. Similarly, I am totally convinced by Evans-Pritchard's argument that the Nuer's life is fundamentally changed by the seasons and all that this implies, or by his point that their dealing with other people is largely dependent on their reckoning of the length of time that has elapsed since they had a common ancestor. However, I am totally sceptical whether the ethnography given by the two authors backs up, in any way, the fundamental claim that these authors seem to make about the conceptualisation of time, these claims which are so similar to those which had been formulated before them by such as Durkheim and Whorf. Most probably when faced with commentators who accused them of cognitive relativism they would feel uncomfortable. Yet, in the way they write, they seem to be presenting their ethnographies as straightforward supporting evidence for these dramatic proposals. This type of ambiguity is typical of much anthropological writing and is an example of the way fundamental claims about human cognition appear and disappear in ethnography as though such matters could be left in mid air.

A cognitive challenge to Munn and Evans-Pritchard

The basic reasons for my scepticism concerning the claims about the conceptualisation of time made in the two books are two. The first is that both writers actually give us evidence that contradicts their unqualified argument about the social and cultural construction of time. The second is that what we know from cognitive psychology makes such claims totally unlikely.

Let us look again at *The Nuer*. On page 222, Evans-Pritchard tells us what happens when neighbouring Dinka are captured and more or less incorporated into Nuer descent groups. He says:

A girl captive is not adopted into the lineage but people say 'caa lath cungni' 'she is given the right to receive bride wealth'. This means that when she is married, or her daughters are married, the sons of the family in which she has been brought up will receive the cattle due to brothers and maternal uncles, and that in return, when the daughters of this family are married, she, or her sons can claim the cow due to the paternal aunt and the cow due to the maternal aunt. (Evans-Pritchard 1940: p. 222)

Now surely it would be impossible to operate such a system with the cyclic understanding of time which Evans-Pritchard claims to exist among the Nuer. The Nuer are anchoring their narrative in a temporality which seems no different from our own and which makes it clear that once an event has happened it is irreversible. Furthermore, the Nuer would never have been able to explain and represent the practice to Evans-Pritchard, something which this passage, containing as it does direct quotations, clearly shows they did, if they had not been able to assume shared temporal implicatures between the producer and the recipient of the information.

Similarly, when we turn to *The Fame of Gawa* we find straightforward evidence that the people of the island think of past, present and future in ways similar to Europeans or anyone else for that matter. To illustrate her point about space–time Munn quotes a Gawa man's following explanation in a passage from a public speech:

[when someone eats a lot of food] it makes his stomach swell: he does nothing but eat (-kam) and lie down (-maisi lie down/sleep); but when we give food (karu) to someone else, when an overseas visitor eats pig, vegetable food, chews betel, then he will take away its noise (buraga-ra), its fame (butu-ra) . . . Gardens and Kula are what makes a man a *guyaw*. Whoever has gardens, overseas visitors come and eat there all the time. They say you are a *guyaw*. [Later they will come and give you armshells and necklaces.] (p. 49)

This narrative shows quite clearly that the man who spoke these words envisaged the pattern of time as a regular irreversible flow. This flow is what makes the explanation of causality he proposes clear. What he is saying is that if you eat your own food at a particular time *then*, at a *later time*, you will merely sleep and *later still* nobody will be impressed, but, if you first grow food, and *then* use it to feast foreigners, *then* your fame will spread, perhaps they will *then* kula with you, which will, in turn, imply that *at an even later time* you will have your gifts returned.

This quotation shows, first of all, that what Munn is talking about is not in any way the cognition of time and space as an organising principle but, instead, what is being referred to is the evocation of space and time *within* a taken-for-granted temporal framework. It is the organising principle of this fixed temporal framework that *enables* him to communicate a meaningful causal sequence to the person he is addressing. As with all forms of human language, the fundamental presuppositions which make the utterance relevant, as is normal, are left unsaid. We are convinced by the Gawa man that the feeding of food to outsiders causes fame precisely because he rightly assumes that the addressee knows that for there to be causality, as Hume would also have reminded us, cause must precede effect within a framework of durability where time is flowing. The absolute categorical necessity of such a presupposition for comprehension is, of course, exactly the point that Kant and after him Durkheim were making when they stressed that the categories of understanding must be, or seem to be, there first, beyond question, *a priori* or non-negotiable. In any case, whatever development takes place these can only be as transformations of a strongly determinist base. If the conceptualisation was not there already, as a framework, the Gawa man could simply say nothing. This point is sufficient to show that the basic claim, apparently made by Munn and the other 'practice theorists' which she cites and does not cite, could not possibly be true in the form in which they are made. The conceptualisation of time cannot be negotiated in practice from moment to moment. This is because a shared conceptualisation of time has to already be in place for practice to occur. The Gawa man can, and does, evoke different times and places; he can explain causality precisely because he can take for granted the non-negotiated conceptual framework of the categories of understanding.

This general point rules out the very strong form of the position taken by Munn which we can just forget about on first principles. It does not, however, rule out the position taken by such as Durkheim, Whorf or Evans-Pritchard. They could argue that they agree that the temporal framework has to be taken for granted for any form of organised social life to take place but that, nonetheless, this framework is 'given' by the particular culture and/or language and varies according to which language or culture we are dealing with. People must treat time *as though* it was beyond question and natural, but we, clever anthropologists, know that it is historical and cultural; in other words relative.

Here, however, another aspect of the quotation discussed actually rules out this traditional anthropological position. It is simply that it is spoken by a Gawa man for the benefit of Nancy Munn, that she seems to have had no difficulty in understanding it, and that, furthermore, she was rightly confident that, if she reproduced the words in English, her readers would also have no difficulty in understanding what was said. This is only possible if we all share the same fundamental categories of understanding. And since the Gawa man and myself have radically different cultural and historical backgrounds and that I, for my part, cannot speak Gawa, it simply means that difference in culture and language is irrelevant for this minimal degree of mutual communication.

Thus Munn's ethnography and that of Evans-Pritchard, far from demonstrating the grandiose propositions of such as Whorf and Durkheim, as it is implicitly claimed they do, actually undermine them drastically. We could leave the matter here, and say that the proposition that the conceptualisation of time is relative has not been proved, or even that internal evidence shows that the contrary conclusion should be reached; but, in fact, it is possible to go much further and to argue that, even if the writers discussed had not given us the conflicting evidence, we should have, nevertheless, been highly suspicious of their claim.

This is because of what we know from experimental studies in cognitive psychology, especially on infants' conceptualisation of time. Implicitly, if not explicitly, all the writers referred to above assume that people *learn* about time and duration. For them, temporal cognition is simply a form of acquired knowledge, since, only if this is so, does it make sense to say that people's fundamental understanding of time comes entirely from history, language, culture, practice or social structure. All the recent evidence, on the other hand, shows that predispositions to understand time in a special way are already largely in place from the moment of birth in humans. There is thus a strong innate element in the cognition of time. This predisposition is a characteristic of normal humans, like having ten fingers. This does not mean that no modification will occur through the process of maturation which builds on that inherited basis, but in the case of temporality the evidence suggests that such modification is much less significant than it is for other areas of cognition. If that is so, to say simply and unhesitatingly that different people have, *at a fundamental level*, totally different and incommensurate concepts of time, as Durkheim, Evans-Pritchard, Munn and many others seem to claim, is tantamount to saying that the people they study belong to different species to themselves.

The history of developmental cognitive psychology has been short but it has been long enough to have undergone a dramatic revolution. Until about twenty years ago the Piagetian view of child development dominated. As we saw in the previous chapter, according to Piaget, children gradually constructed their knowledge of the world, starting from nothing apart from the in-born ability to structure information in ever more complex ways. Evidence in support of such a view was the apparent failure of infants, and even quite old children, to perform a number of basic tasks. As a result, Piaget gave a very slow developmental picture of the child's understanding of time and sequencing (Piaget 1969). Subsequently, this work was shown to have been flawed by the inappropriateness of the experiments for very young infants (Friedman 1990). Recently, a number of ingenious new techniques have revealed that even newborn children already 'know' very much. Particularly relevant here is their presumably innate initial knowledge of naïve physics and arithmetics (Bullock and Gelman 1979; Bower 1989; Baillargeon, Kotovsky and Needham 1995; Spelke, Philips and Woodward 1995). Much of this experimental work is intended to demonstrate other types of competences, usually of a much less fundamental order. However, it also demonstrates the presence in newborn or very young children of a clear understanding that cause must precede effect, that certain rates of movement, for example of a ball rolling behind a screen, govern predictions of when it will appear at the other end, etc. Indeed, the temporal framework implied in all recent work on naïve physics and psychology is so strong and so evident that it is rarely, as such, a subject of much discussion. It seems that not only all humans share this framework but that it is also probably shared with all primates and probably even other animals (Church and Gibbon 1982).

How much is innate and how far this innate starting point is modifiable is open to debate, but it is agreed that the bases of usually totally presupposed temporal understanding forms part of core knowledge and that this scaffolding is already in place as early as it is possible to test for it, i.e. long before it is possible for particular languages or cultures to have any strong effect. This does not mean, of course, that such fundamental early knowledge does not subsequently become enriched or that there is no room for a certain amount of cognitive change though, so far, the evidence seems against such possibility.

As soon as one goes beyond infancy, much more elaborate understanding of time can be demonstrated experimentally but there is no evidence that this is, or could be, fundamentally culturally inflected. Thus two year olds can organise events in sequences for familiar tasks and four year olds can give truly impressive temporal descriptions of familiar activities (O'Connell and Gerard 1985; Nelson 1986). The experimental work has been carried out mainly on Euro-American and Japanese children, but there is no reason to believe that children in other cultural environments are unable to handle sequencing in the way described in these experiments. My own anecdotal observations in a remote part of Madagascar accords with this, even though Malagasy children are much more shy in verbalising their knowledge than are the American children on whom most work so far has been focussed. This is irrelevant, however, since we are dealing here with knowledge that is normally implicit and presuppositional. The basis of the understanding of time is thus clearly based on species-wide shared characteristics.

This psychological work therefore seems to make the absolute claims of such as Durkheim, Whorf or Evans-Pritchard and Munn extraordinarily unlikely. As we saw, these claims could only be squared with propositions of the type that humans in different cultures belong to different species or the equally strange suggestion that there is a stage in the development of children when they suddenly abandon all their early cognitive capacities and replace them by another system learnt from their culture.

With so much experimental work pointing in the same direction, it is not surprising that a common reaction on the part of some of those familiar with the psychological work is to dismiss contemptuously the anthropologists' claims. Thus Steven Pinker, in a way that I have often heard expressed by other cognitive psychologists, considers the Whorfian claims about time and concludes that 'the anthropological anecdotes are bunk' (1995: p. 65). With hardly greater circumspection, Tooby and Cosmides ridicule the 'standard social science model' of cultural variability (Tooby and Cosmides 1992). This is not surprising, as the totalitarian arrogance which the language used implies and the imprecision of the claims of the social scientists mean that the latter have 'asked for it'. We can see how the ignorance on the part of the anthropologists or historians of the psychological work has led them to slide imperceptively into making impossible claims, and how this situation has enabled their opponents, who include many with a natural science bent, to avoid having to consider taking into account, even for a moment, what these other 'softer' and anecdotal disciplines are discussing. We are back with the unhelpful straitjacket of the nature/culture dichotomy.

Relating levels

In this way, a vociferous reaction to the work of anthropologists, in particular, gets created which has no room at all for any attempt at understanding what it was that Durkheim, Whorf, Evans-Pritchard or Munn were talking about. Their opponents argue that they were simply talking about nothing. This is just inconceivable to anyone who has seriously understood or read the work in question. We can easily understand the exasperation manifested towards the dramatic claims made, and I believe it is largely justified given the looseness of the writing, but this should not lead us to forget what the social scientists have said but rather what it should do is to make us want to reformulate the issues so that we abandon impossible positions but then try anew to see how, within a more dynamic framework, we can understand what the anthropologists were talking about. It will then become possible to seek a combination of these different scientific traditions.

What follows is an attempt to suggest how, on the particular topic of time, this might occur. First, however, a certain amount of ground clearing is necessary.

The initial step in such an enterprise is the most fundamental; it is to render more explicit the theoretical framework of both camps. These theoretical frameworks are clearly strongly influenced by the type of data which both sides obtain through the empirical methods they employ.

The anthropological way of going about things

Field working anthropologists using their traditional methods watch people going about their business and listen to what they say among themselves and to the anthropologist. Cognitive psychologists use the results of laboratory tests where people are asked to do tasks aimed at revealing implicit and unexpressed knowledge which underlies practices. These laboratory tasks are usually not the sort of thing that people would do naturally and certainly not in the way they are asked to do them in the experimental context. In both the case of the anthropologists and the cognitive psychologists the information that they are able to obtain is frustratingly limited if one wants to make general claims about big questions such as the rationale of people's thoughts and actions in the world. However, forgetting their limitations, both sides are easily led to argue that the data they dispose of suffices as a legitimate basis for making propositions that go much beyond their possible significance.

We could characterise the classical anthropological argument as being a top to bottom argument where it is assumed that superior levels determine an invisible basic level.

What I mean by the superior levels is simply what the anthropologist can easily observe as life goes on in the places they study. This includes, in the case of the two examples discussed above, institutions and practices such as the Kula, the practice and importance of commensality and hospitality, cattle keeping, transhumance and the type of 'calendars' and genealogies used. The relevance of these institutions and practices for presuppositions concerning the conceptualisation of duration is far from direct and can only be deduced. In a book such as *The Nuer*, it is largely Evans-Pritchard's intuitions concerning the temporal implications of such things as lineage structure or transhumance that are the basis of his claims about Nuer conceptualisation of time. The Kula and commensality are used similarly in the work of Nancy Munn. To this, both authors add rather rare but more explicit statements from informants about the flow of time, the units of time, the effect of time on people, landscape, the state of the world. However, this material also turns out to be in need of speculative deductive interpretation before it can be made to say anything very relevant about the basis of the understanding of time.

Examples of this way of discovering 'concepts of time' in exotic groups are common in the literature. Thus Cunnison, who was a pupil of Evans-Pritchard, claims to discover non-lineal time among the Luapula people who live in what became modern Zambia, because when elders recount the actions of a long ago predecessor to their office they use the first person singular and the present tense of the verbs to describe his actions (Cunnison 1960). Elaborate theories about the recurrence of different 'ages' in Hindu theology have also been claimed to tell us about the 'cognition' of time.

What it is that such anthropologists hope to discover through their interpretation of those phenomena is, however, something absolutely fundamental: the underlying sense of time or of duration which organises cognitive life and therefore all thought and action. In fact, however, as anthropologists do not usually dispose of data about this they somehow hope that by looking at or *through* the superior level at their disposal, that is the institutions, practices and discourses, they will detect the cognitive underpinnings of the minds of the people studied and the Aristotelian categories of their thought.

It is not surprising that such a methodology produces different and varied versions of local cognitions of time since the only real evidence that the anthropologists have access to are more or less explicit statements, and since it is quite obvious that institutions, ways of life and talk are not the same everywhere, this must mean that, according to the logic of this method, even the most fundamental aspects of cognition vary.

The 'practice' stance of someone such as Munn at first appears different from the typical anthropological way of thinking of Evans-Pritchard's book on the Nuer. He assumes that there is a fixed cognitive scaffolding which can be discovered via the institutions of a particular society. Munn appears to reverse this way of thinking when she claims that as actions occur they *create* the framework of cognition. It is as though the actors discovered *post hoc* the cognitive foundations of what they have just done. This does not make much sense. Nancy Munn argues that temporal cognition only emerges in actions and can only be inferred from these. Such a claim mixes up the problems of doing ethnography and describing the subjectivity of people with the theoretical aim of accounting for the sources of cognition and action. The ethnographer has only access to people's practice and it is quite right to point out the embeddedness of cognition in practice, a point to be discussed in chapter 7. This creates a real problem for the ethnographer in that she needs to separate generative principles from a complex living and on-going process. However, this is not the actors' problem since he or she is not in the business of deciphering the cognitive parameters of their own action. In fact, the opposite to Munn's assumption that basic cognitive categories are being created 'on the hoof' must be true. The cognitive parameters must already be in place for any action to take place. Beliefs about commensality, the Kula, the search for fame, must be known already before a man from Gawa can set sail on a Kula expedition. Furthermore, this knowledge implies a totally explicit existing framework of basic understandings, including the understanding of time as an irreversible flow. These are necessary for the actions the ethnographer observes to have occurred, not the other way round.

To sum up, therefore, except for a few variants which evaporate under scrutiny, the anthropological way of going about things is to assume that, via the analysis of what can be observed in field work and especially in the kind of things people say on certain occasions, one can deduce directly the underlying foundation of the cognitive framework of the people studied.

The cognitive scientist's way of going about things

Cognitive scientists such as Pinker, Tooby and Cosmides and others appear to go about things in the very opposite way to the anthropologists. They assume that in the study of the conceptualisation of time what they need to find out will never appear on the surface in what people do or say in a natural setting and they therefore pay little attention to it. They assume that this knowledge is implicit and presuppositional and already in place and that it can only be discovered by experimental methods. These experimental methods remove the subjects from their normal environment and it involves them in doing tasks that they would normally never dream of doing. This is partly because of the need for statistically valid data but more because the parameters of knowledge are normally taken for granted and will only appear in odd environments. There seems to be good reason for such scientific practices. Furthermore, on the basis of data obtained in this way the cognitive psychologists also believe that what the results of their experimental work shows are forms of cognition that are universal, perhaps innately based and which remain largely unchanged throughout life. In the case of the fundamental cognition of time these are probably largely legitimate conclusions although cognitive scientists may recognise that the effect of specific languages means that their findings need to be qualified in minor ways. Also, we should remember that the experimental evidence they base themselves on is mainly from infants and mainly from Euro-American and Japanese infants at that. However, no serious experimentally based evidence has ever been produced, either in cross cultural work or work on adults, which challenges the very general conclusion that the cognition of time is not fundamentally variable.

At first glance, therefore, the two ways of going about things could not be more different either in method or in conclusions. One starts from events occurring naturally, whether these be linguistic or otherwise. The other creates events in the laboratory that would never occur normally. One assumes that time cognition is explicit or at least easily made explicit. The other assumes that the cognition of time is implicit and very difficult to express by the subjects of the enquiry. One usually concludes that there are fundamental cultural differences while the other assumes it has found species-wide regularities. However, in spite of this *prima facie* disparity, both systems may share more than is at first apparent since the anthropological model and the cognitive science model have two fundamental similarities.

First, both models have a single determinant level. This determinant level is assumed to reflect or to command whatever other ones may exist. Determination by one level inevitably means that all levels are homologous and need not be differentiated. Thus, anthropologists can talk of the Nuer sense of time without specifying whether they are referring to perception, explicit theories, cultural institutions, cognition, representations and narratives since all are presumed to be coherent. The cognitive scientists, by contrast, can similarly assume that what is revealed by the inferences made by infants in the tasks asked of them in experimental settings will govern all aspects of mental and social life and that is not only of infants but also of adults. This is because for both anthropologists and cognitive scientists anything relating to time in any one group of people needs be based on a single overarching and single principle.

Secondly, both sides base their very general conclusions about the cognition of time on the very limited information they actually have evidence for. Although the type of evidence at the disposal of the anthropologists and the cognitive scientists is inevitably the limited product of the methods traditionally used by their respective disciplines, both assume that their data is sufficient for understanding aspects of the cognition of time which, in fact, their methods make them unable to take into account.

Anthropologists base themselves on what people say in normal circumstances. They also have evidence how particular social processes and actions are linked to this talk. They have no direct evidence about the inferential processes which underlie and make possible normal action and speech. The cognitive psychologists, for their part, do have experimental evidence concerning the mechanisms of inference, reasoning, perception, etc., but they do not have evidence of the uses to which these mechanisms are put when people go about the business of their lives in the actual and normal social and practical contexts history has created. The problem is that both sides seem to assume that what they know is sufficient for inferring the knowledge they do not have. Both refuse to distinguish levels analytically.

Now, there is absolutely no need for the absolute determinism between levels which is assumed in both scenarios just described. The anthropologist knows about one level but not about the others. The cognitive psychologist knows about one level and not about the others. However, both lots feel satisfied with their limited knowledge because they assume that all levels are homologous. In fact, this would be bizarre since the levels are of a fundamentally different character. We can accept from the anthropologist that, in their explicit narratives, Gawa people evoke different images of space and time than those that would be evoked by people not involved in the Kula. Furthermore, we can also accept that these evocations are changing from moment to moment. However, none of this justifies claiming that fundamental conceptualisations of duration is affected by any of this. We can accept from the psychologists their evidence of inferential processes concerning causation which are revealed in experimental set-ups and take into account suggestions that these are based on an apparently universal underlying conceptualisation of duration which would therefore apply just as much to the Nuer as to anybody else without refusing Evans-Pritchard's ethnography. We can accept Evans-Pritchard's observation that the Nuer are only discursively interested in the past in so far as it explains social distance without this having any implication for what the psychologists tell us. There is no need for the totalising vision which comes from the blunderbuss combination of all levels introduced, almost surreptitiously, within the anthropological discussions considered at the beginning of this chapter as we can reject the equally unwarranted contempt of anthropological work manifested by some cognitive scientists.

And, as soon as we begin to distinguish between levels, something that will be done more fully in the next chapter, we can formulate really interesting, but admittedly difficult, questions. These questions are all about what connects such different levels since we know that they need to be related because that is how people live their lives. The writers considered above cannot focus on the relation between levels because they do not distinguish them. On the other hand, considering both the work of cognitive scientists and that of anthropologists and other social scientists enables us to ask these new and important questions. Thus, trying to understand the coexistence of the different levels is what the rest of this chapter will focus on.

Imagination and time travel

One way of understanding the connection between levels is reflecting on the specifically human capacity for imagination. This is because it involves the level which anthropologists are often drawn to because of the type of data they are familiar with and which they often mistake for the framework of all aspects of cognition. There may well be rudimentary forms of the capacity for imagination in other species but it is beyond doubt that the potential for imagination is developed much more extensively in *Homo sapiens* than in other animals (Suddendorf and Corballis 1997; Whiten and Suddendorf 2007).

Imagination is a huge subject but two aspects are particularly relevant here. The first is our capacity for what psychologists have called 'time travel'. Time travel enables us to remember, and, to a certain extent, experience, past events of our lives and to imagine future events in which we may be involved. Whether the ability for time travel depends on language is a much-debated point especially now that it has been claimed that other species too have the capacity for time travel. We use time travel for all sorts of things, some more mundane than others, ranging from planning in making a list of what to buy in a supermarket, to recalling past episodes of our lives, or the evoking of the past and the future in myth and poetry.

Time travel is of relevance for the present discussion because what Munn presents as evidence for the exotic character of Gawa time is precisely a use of this human-wide time travel capacity. The man who she quotes and whose statement I discuss above is engaging in time travel, as he imagines prospectively what will happen on future Kula journeys and, as he engages in time travel retrospectively, when he remembers previous Kula journeys.

There is thus nothing unusual in what the Gawa man is doing; he is simply using the capacity for imagination which characterises our species. Once we realise this, it becomes clear that such a capacity tells us absolutely nothing specific or unusual about the conceptualisation of time in Gawa. Time travel does not modify our core cognition because what happens when we use this capacity is phenomenologically parenthesised. We are aware that the images of past and future are acts of imagination where, to a certain extent, and to a certain extent only, normal rules of time and space are temporally suspended (Clayton and Russell 2009).Time travel is something which we can do because we have the ability to use our brain for alternative scenarios than the ones in which we presently are. As normal people engage in time travel in their imagination, they do not muddle up the past and the future with the present. Indeed, doing so is a sign of serious neurological problems and negates the very point of time travel. Paul Harris and his associates, contradicting earlier work by Piaget, have shown that even very young children can keep stories about characters such as super heroes quite separate from what they consider reality and, furthermore, these stories can negate our basic understandings of time, as in science fiction, without this fact changing our conceptualisation of time in any way when it comes to be used for practical purposes. This is because children keep these stories in a distinct 'box' where some rules are suspended. Indeed, the ability to engage in time travel competently requires a robust ability to realise that what is being evoked is not the here and now (Harris 2000).[6] And, of course, we retain the ability to time travel in adulthood and develop it. Imagination thus enables us to live in other worlds while knowing that these are not the here and now. This ability is what is used in fiction, poetry and other creative activities, whether these are artistic or scientific. Most importantly, for the topics which have most concerned social anthropology and this chapter, the ability to imagine other worlds lies at the very root of human social life.

Recognising that we have the ability to indulge in imagination is not in itself sufficient for grasping what is going on in actual situations where humans are involved. The universality of the ability to indulge in time travel does not mean that it is used in the same way or even to the same extent in all groups of people and at all times. These uses of imagination are what anthropologists so often present to us as data of the cognition of time. Thus, as so many anthropologists have stressed, it is true that hunters and gatherers, or Amerindians, do not frequently engage in long-term time travel and this has no doubt the economic and social implications these writers have so successfully discussed (Woodburn 1982; Gow

---

[6] Piaget greatly underestimated the ability of young children to keep different levels separate, that we can imagine scenarios within which certain intuitive understandings are suspended or replaced.

2001). Again, there is no reason not to be convinced when Evans-Pritchard tells us that Nuer time travel towards the past is directed by the implications of their kinship system. These facts, however, do not give us access to the Nuer's conceptualisation of time in general but it does tell us about the kind of images that they are likely to evoke in imaginative time travel.

It is clear that the capacity for imagination and time travel has crucial significance for human cognition. There is, however, an area where it is particularly important for understanding the nature of human society and its relation to the temporal aspects of imaginative evocations.

One thing that normal human children do, irrespective of culture, and which chimpanzees do not do, is engage in what has been called pretend play. From the age of about eighteen months to two years human children begin to play at pretending that one thing is another; the example often given is that of a child getting hold of a banana and pretending that it is a telephone. Unlike what Piaget believed, it has been quite conclusively shown that this is not because the child is muddled but because it is fun. The child has therefore the ability to handle two, or perhaps even more, registers simultaneously and to act within them, each in different ways, distinguishing them and even enjoying their non-identity. Children are able to keep the make believe world quite apart from that of ordinary practice, as has been shown by a whole range of experiments (Harris and Kavanaugh 1993; Rakoczy and Tomasello 2006). As the child develops, pretend play becomes, in some cases, very elaborate (see Harris 2000: ch. 2). Two- and three-year-old Malagasy girls, for example, use corn cobs as pretend babies and young boys herd 'cattle' that are, in fact, clay models they have just made. It is absolutely clear to any observer that the children are well aware of the fact that these are not real babies or real cattle. Very soon, this pretend play becomes complex and involves shared pretend games. Several types of teacher and pupil games are common in the western world and are often given as examples of this. In Madagascar, too, I have often witnessed and photographed groups of children playing together at mock rituals such as funerals. It is particularly relevant for the topic of this chapter that these games and pretences occur within a parenthesised time and space world which is understood to be so by the participants. This makes the acts of imagination competently and fluently manipulable by the children.

Imagination and social roles

Rakoczy has pointed out how pretend play, as it develops in children, might be a learning ground for much more complex social skills (Rakoczy 2008). Like myself (Bloch 2008), he has drawn attention to the significance of pretend play for the child's understanding of that crucial aspect of all human society, which is the existence of roles such as 'father', 'professor' or 'queen'. This is because for a child to play 'teacher' when she is aware that she is not the teacher requires that she understands the role 'teacher' as separate from the individual who she knows as her teacher, and understands that this role can be attributed to different individuals irrespective of their identity.

The separateness of roles from the empirical carrier is a characteristic not only of pretend play but also of adult social life and in realms which are not considered as play. This is the case for such roles as 'citizen', 'president', 'pupil', 'professor', etc. The similarity between roles in pretend play and in serious life makes it clear that the very idea of role is a matter of imagination since it does not relate to an empirical aspect of the persons who are endowed with the role. The person in front of you can be a 'student' without this being marked by any empirical feature. Nobody expects that it need be, showing how at ease we are with operating in imaginative worlds at the very same time as we are aware and act towards the presence of a non-imaginary world, that of the empirical person to whom the role has been attributed. We can thus choose for the 'student' a seat near a window because we have noted that he has poor eyesight. We easily and continually understand the existence of parallel worlds of which there are different expectations without this coexistence causing any confusion. The same is true for identities which come from 'imagined' group membership, such as belonging to a nation (Anderson 1983). Being French, for example, is understood by all to be an imaginary phenomenon in the sense that anybody who believes it is necessary to find an empirical mark of frenchness on the body of those who consider themselves, and who are considered by others to be French, would be stupid. Of course, the people concerned would probably not use the word imagination to explain this understanding since in English it carries the implication of falsity, but they would have no doubt that being French is not of the same order of reality as having a broken leg. In other words, they, like all of us, have and use this essential human capacity to operate competently and simultaneously on different registers without getting confused.

There is a further element that needs to be added to this analysis of the imaginary aspect of such things as roles and groups. Engaging in this type of social imagination in the non-playful adult world is a totally different matter from that of the individual imagination of a lone child playing with a spoon and calling it 'mummy'. Such pretend play does also involve imagining the role of mummy, but the child can suddenly decide that the spoon is after all nothing but a spoon, or even that it is a 'daddy'. This is not the case with the role 'policeman', for example, and this lack of individual choice is an essential aspect of social roles in adult life which derives from the fact that we are dealing with *joint and shared* imagination. Rakoczy has stressed this aspect of the more elaborate forms of pretend play. They involve the co-ordination of imagination of several or many individuals. When we think of the descent groups of the Nuer or the fame of the people engaged in the Kula in Gawa, it is clear that we are also dealing with the co-ordinated imaginations of the Nuer or of the people of Gawa. Because of this shared character, the imagining of roles and groups and other shared imagination takes on a much less personal character than the term 'imagination' normally suggests. Indeed, refusing to accept to participate in such joint imaginings is a threat to all and will most probably be harshly punished. The child may thus be predisposed for pretend play but very soon this predisposition will be harnessed and recruited in already created scenarios which have quite different implications because of their shared character.

The use of shared imagination for creating the phenomenological reality of roles and corporate groups is crucial for our understanding of social life. It is particularly relevant here since it concerns the topic of time. Groups and roles as such and as they are imagined have the oddity of having a kind of permanence through time which contrast with the continual mutability of the empirical which I have elsewhere called 'transactional'. This relative stability is made possible because of their non-empirical character. Thus, being a citizen is an unchanging aspect of anyone who is a citizen; it is not relevant to the status 'citizen' whether the person concerned has a cold, is wearing a wig or even if she is dead. The great significance of this defiance of time in the very notion of role becomes evident when we consider the example of groups. It is possible to say and to imagine that the French, as a nation, 'exist since the sixth century and have survived many trials and tribulations' while, of course, everybody understands that it is not the actual living people who have somehow vanquished death but their imaginary 'roles' and 'groups'.

These time-defying imagined groups and roles have yet another most important characteristic. They seem to form systems, though whether these systems are as systematic as they are believed to be by the people who participate in imagining them is an open question. Very large parts of what social anthropologists were studying in the mid-twentieth century are elements of these imaginary 'systems'. Following Leach and his discussion of what he calls stereotypic models (Leach 1954: p. 286), I have suggested elsewhere that this is what is indicated by such labels as 'social structure' (Bloch 1977) or religion (Bloch: 2008) or ideology. These are shared imaginary systems rather than the straightforward 'social systems' that early anthropologists believed them to be. Searle, for his part, has called these systems 'institutional reality' and he stresses how they include in their nets other institutional imaginations like bank notes which are understood, as they are used, both to have non-empirical value and to be merely bits of paper (Searle 1995). Most importantly, as we shall see below, it is not very surprising that, like their constituents, groups and roles, they, as a totality, create 'time'-defying regimes whose existence is in imagination.

An example of this are the statements made by the anonymous Nuer on which Evans-Pritchard based himself in the discussion of Dinka captives which was quoted above. In this, he tells us what happens to Dinka girls when they are caught; he then goes on to tell us which type of relative (maternal uncles) should receive bridewealth, and which should give it. As we listen to him, we realise that he is talking about a complex system of interrelated rules, rights and duties, not of people. Such an institutional system has to be impersonal; it concerns the interactions of roles and groups in an organised structure; it is not about the relations of actual individual people. The evoked imagined system concerns Dinka girl captives not any particular girl; it concerns maternal uncles not any particular person. Inevitably, since the system is made of imaginary entities, it too is a creation of imagination. It is also a normative system which, like a legal code, has to apply irrespective of person or circumstances. And it is only because it consists of imaginary entities that are time defying that the system itself appears to have permanence which negates the fluidity of life. We find therefore that the shared imaginations of permanent roles enable human society to appear to be regulated by systems which transcend them. It is the system of rules and duties, norms and values that we misleadingly say 'organises' society. The system can only do this by creating other systems of time representations which such anthropologists as Evans-Pritchard have been tempted to represent as exotic while in fact they may just be an aspect of what is necessary for all societies to function.

Of course, these shared imaginations also lead to very practical activities such as fighting among the Nuer or going on dangerous sea journeys among the people of Gawa but the practical side of things is kept quite separate. As Malinowski long ago pointed out, practical actions have to be regulated by our implicit understandings, above all of time. These are species-wide psychological features because they have been adapted by evolution to the world as it is.

We therefore find that the Nuer and the people of Gawa are able to handle at least two levels simultaneously; an everyday level which is largely taken for granted and is governed by a conceptualisation of time which is little different from that used by all of mankind. This is implicit and it is what the cognitive psychologists study, and which they reveal by their methods. The Nuer and the people of Gawa also handle another most important system which exists in imagination and which consists of norms, institutions, roles, death defying groups and legal systems. This level involves alternative temporal implications which, although ultimately built up by a system of transformations (often ritual in character) from the implicit species-wide basic level, seems to deny it. This imaginary system is usually explicit and easy to put into words by the people studied and by the anthropologist. It thus becomes the level that anthropologists concentrate on and which supplies misleading illustrations of exotic temporalities.

In conclusion, it turns out that the quarrels between anthropologists and cognitive scientists are based on nothing more than the fact that they have been looking at different things and they have pretended that they were the same. The people of Gawa and the Nuer, on the other hand, like people everywhere, live in a world which involves a variety of levels, and they have the ability that they developed as infants to live competently within several levels at once, more particularly in shared imaginary systems. The fact that the people we study can perform this feat is the best justification there is for the need for co-operation by both types of disciplines since their different methods enable us to grasp these different aspects. However, we can go further and try theoretically to put together the different types of findings, and as we do this we gain new insights which neither type of discipline could reach alone. This I have attempted to show in the discussion about the role of imagination which has concluded this chapter. The attempt to relate such different levels, some of which are best studied by cognitive scientists, some of which are best studied by traditional anthropologists, will also be the subject of the next chapter.

SIX

ᘛ

Reconciling social science and cognitive science notions of the 'self'

The preceding chapter has shown that the combination of studies produced by anthropologists with those of other cognitive scientists such as psychologists or neurologists seems, at first, impossible since what they propose appears contradictory. However, we saw that if we introduce the notion of different yet interconnected levels the apparent contradiction disappears and a richer picture is revealed. This chapter continues the argument that such an approach is also valuable when it is applied to the very core of our studies: that is what makes human individuals. Again we shall see that what appears at first as incompatible conclusions emanating, on the one hand, from psychologists and neurologists and, on the other, from social and cultural anthropologists, becomes, when theoretically combined, a dynamic whole.

The history of the social sciences and especially that of modern anthropology has been dominated by a recurrent controversy about what kind of phenomenon people are. On the one hand, there are those who assume that human beings are a straightforward matter. They are beings driven by easily understood desires directed towards an empirically obvious world. The prototypical examples of such theoreticians are Adam Smith, Herbert Spencer or more recently the proponents of rational choice theory. These early social science theories have also been the assumptions underlying most cognitive science; in some cases this has been quite explicit (Tooby and Cosmides 1990; Boyd and Richerson 2005). By contrast, these positions have been criticised, again and again, by many modern social scientists, more particularly social and cultural anthropologists. They have stressed that in theory there can be no place for actors who are simply imagined as 'generic human beings' since people are always the specific product of their particular and unique location in the social, the historical and the cultural process. Among the writers who have made this kind of point are Durkheim, Dumont and more recently Michel Foucault and the post-modernists.

Anthropologists have tended to be on the side of the latter because they like to use their knowledge of exotic societies to argue that what the others see as 'human nature' is merely the western person glorified. Such a point is often justified, but the 'culturalists' rarely go on to answer the very difficult questions which would follow: how far do they want their argument to go? Is there really nothing to be said about the species *Homo sapiens*?

The anthropological challenge has, once again, not gone unanswered, again most vocally in the work of Pinker (2002). The anti-anthropological writers stress the general aspects of such things as human cognitive development. However, this is usually done without having paid more than lip service to the cultural construction of people.

This is because the critics of the anthropologists are cognitive scientists such as psychologists and analytic philosophers with very little understanding of what motivates anthropologists in the first place. A few scholars such as Sperber and myself have seriously attempted the reconciliation that his book seeks (Sperber 1996).

The back and forth between anthropological culturalists and scientific universalists in the attempt to specify human beings is in the end tiresome. It is one more manifestation of the nature/culture impasse. As we saw in chapters 2 and 3, the theoretical history of the social sciences has repeated itself far too often. We seem never to get anywhere since both sides seem to have good reason for arguing that the other is wrong without being able to incorporate the aspects of their opponents' argument which they usually also recognise, but only in passing, as partially valid.

The reason for this continual repetition of old controversies is due to the ease with which both sides can criticise the other by pointing to the unreality of their opponents' understanding of people. The culturalists can point to the abstraction of disembodied *a priori* entities such as the rational actor of game theory, or the culturally free, history free, creatures of much psychology and philosophy. The universalists can ridicule the equally bodiless and mindless creatures of much cultural anthropology, where people are seen as nothing other than epiphenomena of specific places and times.

In what follows, I argue that the cause for the endless repetition of controversy, in the social sciences at least, comes from the inability to consider what we are talking about as a natural organism rather than as an abstraction of unclear ontological status. If we focus on the human animal, the product of an evolution which has made us a very special being, which is not ontologically different from other living species, we can begin the job of understanding the complex way in which we are simultaneously created by our biology, which includes our psychology, and by history and culture, without getting lost in the smoke of battle of the fantasy wars of nature/culture. If we do this, social scientists can think together with the other cognitive sciences. Then social scientists can explain to psychologists, neurologists and philosophers in a more convincing way how much they need to seriously take into account the social and the cultural. My purpose here is to change the ground over which the old controversies have been fought to a manageable one where the different disciplines can meet and engage in a joint, yet difficult enterprise.

The topic of what kind of phenomenon human beings are is where the apparently irresoluble conflict between the 'universalists' and the 'culturalists' seems most intense. This matter is indicated in the social and cognitive sciences when terms such as self, the I, agent, subject, person, individual, dividuals, identity, etc., are used. These terms all involve the attempt to describe what it is to be oneself and what we assume others to be, in this or that place (The problematic distinction between self-understanding and the representation of others is usually unexamined in most of the social science literature as opposed to what is the case in the cognitive sciences.)

The lumping together of these different terms may well seem to be inappropriate by social scientists, even sloppy, since many authors take great pain in distinguishing these words and offering extremely precise definitions. The problem, however, comes when we try to put together this massive literature; when, for example, we try to relate Geertz's discussion of the Balinese 'person' (1973), with Dumont's 'individual' (1983), Mauss's 'moi' (1938) and Rosaldo's 'self' (1984).[1] When I attempt such combination I have to admit that I am completely lost and so I will refer to this entire indistinct galaxy, some part of which, or all of which, these terms seem to refer to, simply as the 'blob'. This seems particularly justified since, in spite of this multiplicity of would-be distinct labels, much the same claims have been made, whichever word is used.

Foremost among the claims made by anthropologists is the proposition that the blob is fundamentally culturally and/or historically variable. This is what anthropologists mean when they say that there is no such thing as human nature, a proposition which poses the general epistemological problem of what then we are dealing with. If this were so, of course, if the blob was totally variable, moulded by history and culture, then it would be nothing at all, just an arbitrary category of our culture, one that groups under various ethnocentric labels things that have nothing *essentially* to do with each other. If so, the blob, under whatever labels it masquerades, would not be a suitable subject for theoretical study.

This, however, is a conclusion that, in spite of their general predilection for radical cultural determinism, seems not to be taken very seriously by

---

[1] André Beteille expresses the same frustration (Beteille 1991: p. 251).

anthropologists. When anthropologists actually get down to specifics, we usually find much less ambitious propositions. Thus, it is not usually proposed that there are as many blobs as there are cultural variations but rather that there are two kinds of blobs in the world. Sometimes this point is expressed generally, as a contrast between the modern or western blob, on the one hand, and the blob of the rest of mankind, on the other. This is, for example, what Durkheim argued in *The Division of Labour in Society* (1893) with his distinction between organic and mechanical solidarity.

Similarly, Dumont (1983) stresses the same familiar dualist contrast of the individualism of the post-Reformation west, with the holism of the hierarchical rest. The same dichotomy is also found in the work of ethnographers or historians who, although they talk about particular places, argue that there, or then, the self, the person, the subject, or what have you, is different from what 'we', in the modern west, have here and/or now. Thus, Wood (2008) argues that the very notion of self was absent in biblical times, Snell in the Iliad (1953), Marilyn Strathern argues that the New Guinea person is quite different from the western one (1988), Kondo (1990) argues this for the Japanese self, McKim Marriot and Inden for India (1977), Geertz for Bali (1973), etc. The west seems simply used as the contrast to the specific situations discussed, but, in fact, it turns out that these very varied non-western non-modern places are very similar among themselves, places where interiority and individuality is devalued but where social relationships and group membership dominate. More recently, a further twist has been added with some writers arguing that in post-modernity we have now arrived at a post-blob, post-modern, stage (Ewing 1990; Markus and Kitiyama 1991). This addition might be thought to lead to a tripartite division with pre-blob, blob and post-blob but in fact the proposed pre-modern blob and the post-modern blob look singularly alike in that they are both non-essentialist, distributed, contextual and divided. Anthropological arguments about the blob can therefore be summarised as saying there is a great and absolute divide between the individualist west and the social relational rest.

The basis for the repeated exhortation that we should not assume, as the universalists do, that what *we* know as the blob is applicable everywhere is real enough. It is a common experience of ethnographers who work in very different societies and cultural milieus, such as me, to go no further, to be struck and indeed even sometimes shocked, by how little value is given to individual motivations and how roles and group membership are the main, and often the only expressed, criteria of right conduct. This is also reflected in certain non-modern, non-western legal codes such as those on which Mauss based himself in his discussion of the concept of the person, or in the implications of rituals, such as those discussed by Marilyn Strathern, which she uses as the basis of her analysis of the Melanesian dividuals (Strathern 1988). Such data does seem to produce a view of people as merely points in social systems while their internal states, their intentions, their absolute individuality and personal desires are irrelevant. This dichotomous contrast between the west and these 'other' societies is often exaggerated (Leenhardt 1985; Parry 1989; Beteille 1991). However, there are very real and important differences between cultures which are worth discussing. Thus, it is not my intention to minimise the significance of the 'cultural' as it is argued for in the works I have been implicitly or explicitly referring to, but instead to ask whether the facts that have been noted have the fundamental implications for the 'construction' of the blob that so many social scientists give them. I argue below that they do not. This, however, simply means that we have to integrate the work of anthropologists with that of cognitive scientists; we must place the anthropological ideas *within* a model that is not antagonistic, but compatible, with what cognitive sciences can teach us.

Two anthropological writers have already called into question the excesses of the relativist position in relation to the blob, especially when it goes under the name of 'self'. Melford Spiro in a devastating critique of authors such as McKim Marriot, Geertz and others demonstrates how the evidence used for such dramatic generalisations is selective (1993). As an example, he notes that reference to the devaluation of the self in Theravada Buddhism is not, as has been suggested, evidence of the absence of the notion in a country such as Burma, but, rather, of its presence. In a somewhat similar vein Naomi Quinn (2006) criticizes recent post-modern writing in anthropology that suggests that the idea of the integrated self is outdated and/or wrong on the weak and trivial basis of the uncontroversial fact that people can hold contradictory ideals. Her point is that explicit reflexive self-representation cannot be equated with the blob as it is lived and, putting the words in her mouth that I will use below, that we must distinguish cognition and meta-representation, that is re-representations, in these cases public re-representations, about cognition (Sperber 2000). These meta-representations are made possible through the use of imagination, as was discussed in the last chapter. (I am, however, much more hesitant than she is, given our present state of knowledge, in identifying various aspects of selfhood directly with different types of functional or anatomical areas of the brain.)

Spiro and Quinn make two convincing and important criticisms of the work of anthropologists: first, they are right that anthropological writing about the blob is often spectacularly imprecise and, secondly, it is true that claims made in this area are commonly of very uncertain epistemological status. I also support explicitly Quinn's implicit argument that the attempt at naturalising what is being talked about would help clear the fog (Quinn 1969).

The implication of the critiques by Spiro and Quinn is that anthropologists are wrong when they make the absolutist claim that the blob is simply a product of history and is totally culturally variable. Neither author, however, claims that what they indicate by the words 'culture' and 'society' do not have an influence, but the question how, and how far this is so, cannot be advanced until the epistemological status of what is claimed is clarified. Thus, as both Spiro and Quinn recognise, it is not that anthropologists are talking about nothing in their discussions of self, person, agent, personality, identity, but that what it is they are talking about is not clear, and how far they want to go cannot be pinned down.

As Spiro and Quinn have done a good job in criticising much anthropological writing, this clears the way for a more positive attempt at replacing the anthropology within the wider theory they implicitly call for. What follows is the attempt to do this.

Distinguishing and relating levels

One major problem in social science writing is the lack of any serious attempt to distinguish levels in the phenomena to which the blob words seem to refer. It is true that some anthropological writers do make a weak attempt at distinguishing levels but these are soon forgotten. Thus, Mauss begins his essay on the self and/or the person in the following way: 'I [shall not] speak to you of psychology . . . it is plain . . . that there has never existed a human being who has not been aware, not only of his body, but also, at the same time, of his individuality, both spiritual and physical, . . . My subject is entirely different . . . the notion that men in different ages have formed of [the self]' (Mauss 1985: p. 3). Yet the essay continues as a discussion of his 'first subject'. Similarly, though the other way round, Antze and Lambek state in a book about culture and memory that autobiographical memory 'and the "self" or "subject" mutually imply one another' (Antze and Lambek 1996: p. xxi), but we then find that they slide away from a discussion of the central issue by telling us that 'our book is less about memory than about "memory" . . . That is to say it is about how the very idea of memory comes into play in society and culture' (Antze and Lambek 1996: p. xv). This presumably refers to local ethno-psychological theories about whose value they do not commit themselves. Mauss says that he will not talk of psychology but does, while Antze and Lambek declare they will but don't and, instead, talk of what I shall call below meta-representations.

Distinguishing levels of the blob is very difficult but essential if we are to understand the relation of the blob in general to the blob in particular historical and geographical locations. Few things have more hindered dialogue between social and cognitive sciences than proper consideration of what level we are dealing with and of the significance of the relation between these levels.

What follows is, therefore, a rough attempt at distinguishing levels in the natural phenomenon because this is necessary for understanding how social science, and especially anthropological discussions concerning the blob, can be integrated with those from the cognitive sciences. Interestingly, distinguishing levels also produces a kind of natural history of what I have called above 'the lower levels' of the blob which are characterised by features that we may assume are inherited from our very remote premammalian ancestors since these are shared with other distant living species. Other levels, here qualified as 'higher', are unique specialisations of our species. The integration of anthropological considerations within the wider framework outlined here thus also suggests a facilitation of the integration of the social science theories within evolutionary theory (Seeley and Sturm 2006: p. 321ff).

The following preliminary attempt at distinguishing levels is based on the work of a number of scholars in cognitive science who tend to employ one of the names used to indicate the blob: the self. Relying on these authors is, however, a tricky enterprise since they are not all in agreement either. Fortunately, for the simple purposes of the present exercise, it is possible to by-pass most of the disagreements by concentrating on what nearly all are agreed on. What is crucial is that there indeed *are* very different levels to the blob, with the deepest levels shared by all living things and the highest levels creating the possibility of a narrative reflexive autobiography. It is essential, however, to remember that all the levels one might choose to distinguish are simply points in what is a continuum, which means that they are all related to each other even though some are more directly affected by specificities of time and place while others

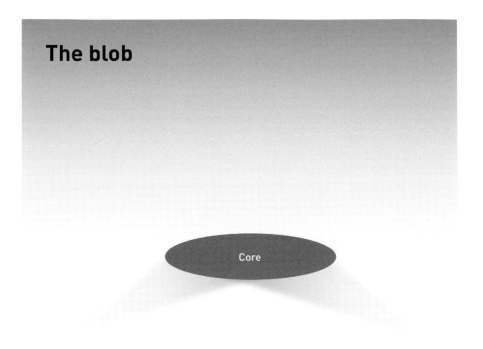

The blob

Core

FIGURE 1.

are not. All those involved in the discussions are agreed that somewhere in that progression language and reflexivity, meta-cognition or meta-representation come into play (e.g. Neisser 1988; Damasio 1999).

The list of levels noted below simply 'will do' for the purpose at hand and will not probably cause relevant problems for my argument, although the issues are greatly simplified and the terms used very loosely.

First of all we can distinguish a level that has often been labelled the 'core self' (see Figure 1). Some aspects of this are very general indeed. These involve two things (1) a sense of ownership and location of one's body, (2) a sense that one is author of one's own actions (Vogeley and Fink 2003; David, Newen and Vogeley 2008). This type of selfhood must be shared by all animate creatures since, as Dennett puts it, even a lobster who relishes claws must know not to eat its own (Dennet 1991: p. 429).

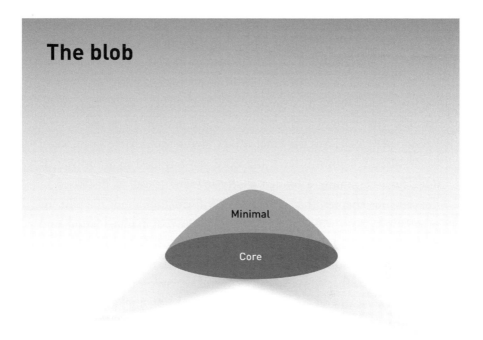

The blob

Minimal

Core

FIGURE 2.

(I suspect that even the most dedicated cultural relativist is unlikely to argue that this level varies from one human group to another.) It should be noted that the word 'sense', as I have applied it to this level, is used here in a particularly thin way, implying no reflexive awareness whatsoever. However, it must also be stressed that, even at this level, we are dealing with quite complex cognition as Descartes's discussion of phantom limbs long ago emphasised, and also as is shown experimentally by more recent work, such as those with the 'rubber hand' where a subject can be made to feel sensations in a model arm (Botvinick and Cohen 1998).

Above this level is one often labelled the 'minimal self' (see Figure 2). This involves a sense of continuity in time. Many animals from crows to chimpanzees have this sense of their own continuity and they, like us, attribute a similar continuity in time to their con-specifics (Hauser,

Kralik, Botto-Mahan, Garrett and Oser 1995). This sense of continuity in time is essential for the use of any type of longer-term memory and seems essential for more advanced cognition such as the ability of self-recognition, demonstrated, for example, in recognising oneself in a mirror. Animals such as chimpanzees and gorillas can do this. Interestingly, this sense of continuity of oneself and others is particularly developed in social species (Emery and Clayton 2004). Here again, when we are dealing with this level, the word sense is used in a thin way. It does, however, imply a limited ability to 'time travel' as discussed in the previous chapter, that is the use of information about the past for present behaviour which enables 'being' in the past in imagination, and the ability to plan future behaviour which requires 'being' in the future in imagination. Nonetheless, this ability implies no reflexive awareness of the mental state that one is in. It does, however, involve episodic memory and it involves the retention of some such episodic memories without these being necessarily woven into a coherent autobiography.

Conscious access requires a higher stage which I call here, with great hesitation, following a number of authors, 'the narrative self' (Humphrey and Dennett 1989; Dennett 1992) (see Figure 3). (I am uncomfortable with the word narrative in that it suggests that people necessarily go in for elaborate narratives about themselves, while, as will be made clear below, this does not necessarily occur. However, because the word narrative has been so widely used I feel obliged to retain it. (See Strawson for an argument against narrativity (2005).) The narrative self is closely linked with autobiographical memory. Thus, Tulving tells us that the narrative self and autobiographical memory imply each other (Tulving 1985). This association is not problematic yet it suggests an important modification of the idea of autobiographical memory as it is usually presented in the literature. This modification comes from the fact that the narrative self, as I use the term here, is only one level of the blob and that, although the levels can be distinguished heuristically, in reality they merge into each other. This means that the narrative self is not independent of the lower

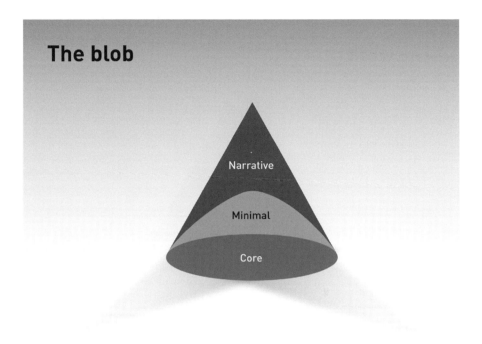

The blob

Narrative

Minimal

Core

FIGURE 3.

levels and, if this is so for the narrative self this means it is also so for autobiographical memory while the use of this phrase suggests, wrongly to my mind, a free standing system. The distinction between the levels discussed so far is not discontinuous and these are not fully separable. We are dealing with a continuum (see Figure 4). The implications of this for social science are very great and I will return to them below. However, before this can be done further clarification is necessary.

Difficult questions about autobiographical memory and the narrative self revolve around whether these are normally accessible to consciousness, how far these require language and how far they can be equated with the stories that people *actually* tell about themselves (Bloch 1998; Nelson 2003).

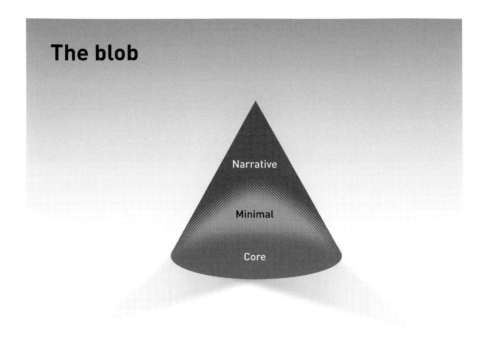

The blob

Narrative

Minimal

Core

FIGURE 4.

Some authors, such as Dennett (1992) and Ricoeur (1985), have argued that this level necessarily implies consciousness, language and the ability to tell stories about oneself, in other words explicitly expressed auto-biographical memory. The difficulty with the notion of the 'narrative self' comes precisely from this lumping together of different elements. Need the autobiography of autobiographical memory be conscious or merely consciously accessible? Do autobiographical memory and the 'narrative self' require language and, if not, is there not a non-linguistic narrative self, to be distinguished from a linguistic level? How far are we dealing with cognition or meta-cognition, with representations or meta-representations? In other words, is having an autobiography the same thing as being aware that one has an autobiography? Is talking about one's autobiographical past the same as having and using such an autobiographical memory? A capacity, which, it is most likely, we share with non-linguistic anthropoids.

These difficulties have been highlighted by the philosopher Galen Strawson in his discussion of the notion of the 'narrative self' (Strawson 2005). He argues that there are some people who are into creating conscious explicit autobiographical narratives about themselves, these he calls 'diachronics', and others, like himself, who are just not interested in doing this. It is not their rhetorical style. They do not see appropriate occasions for talking about themselves. He calls these latter people 'episodics'.

Strawson argues that one should separate those who merely manifest an 'episodic' self, which does not involve a conscious and explicit expression of the kind of autobiography that one would talk about in natural circumstances, from those who manifest a 'diachronic' self, who have a strong sense of having a narrative autobiographical self or an 'I that is a mental presence now, was there in the past, and will be there in the future.' Such people are most likely to go on about it and not wanting to do so is not a sign that one is a deficient member of the human race (Strawson 1999: p. 109) (see Figure 5).

Strawson talks of two different types of people but this is so at the phenomenological level only. However, I would argue that, in terms of the constitution of the blob, both lots, in spite of different outward behaviour, have the level which I awkwardly have to call the narrative self. However, only some people, Strawson's diachronics, have an extra. They engage in a particular form of activity which involves creating a meta-representational diachronic narrative self by talking about their feelings, their inner states and their autobiography. This meta-representational extra is enabled by the human capacity for imagination discussed in the last chapter and is expressed in explicit linguistic acts but relies on institutionalised situations where this kind of expressed introspection appears appropriate. An example would be psychoanalysis. A more

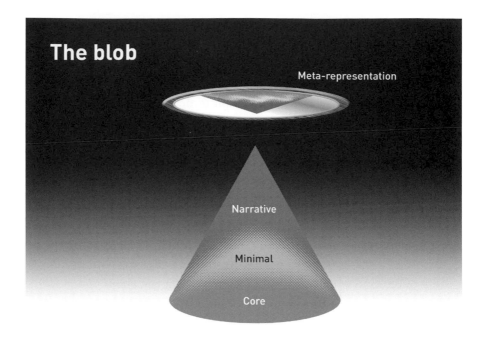

FIGURE 5.

indirect product of such meta-representations is involved in the shared imaginations of roles and corporate groups. As a phenomenon, this is situated between, on the one hand, the individual and un-institutionalised imaginations of young children engaged in pretend play or the adult creating stories such as science fiction and, on the other, the institutionalised and widely shared imaginary systems of corporate groups and roles.

If that is so, Strawson is thus suggesting an answer to questions which are often muddled together in anthropology and elsewhere. The stories that some people tell about themselves or about the nature of selves in their cultures are a quite different matter to whether they have the level which I had to call here the narrative self. Everybody has a narrative self in the sense I use the term. Some people go in for meta-representing this (see

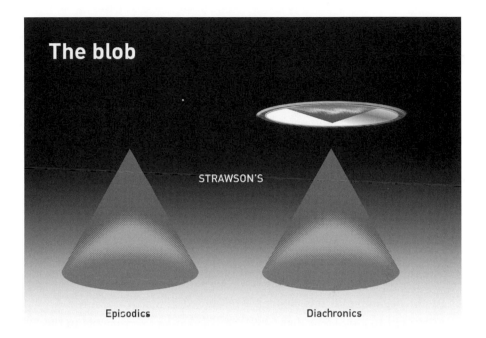

The blob

STRAWSON'S

Episodics   Diachronics

FIGURE 6.

Figure 6). Only some do not, or do so much less because, as Zahavi puts it, 'we should not make the mistake of confusing the reflective, narrative grasp of a life with the pre-reflective experiences that make up that life prior to the experiences being organised into a narrative' (Zahavi n.d.).

The difference between Strawson's two types of people is thus much less fundamental than the differences in levels that I have been discussing so far. The fact that diachronics go in for meta-representations of themselves may be considered as a quite different matter to the constitution of the blob. Explicit narrative rhetorical manifestations are public acts and as such are determined by the social and cultural context in which they occur. This is a different matter. It was discussed already in the previous chapters. However, even though if at the level of explicit discourse Strawson's diachronics and episodics will appear very different in that they will sometimes talk about different things and possibly sometimes act in different ways, this does not mean that they belong to quasi different species; in fact the difference is one of rhetorical style. This distinction between the expressed and the non-expressed narrative self becomes clear when we distinguish what people are like and what they talk about. This applies equally to autobiographical memory. It too has a double aspect. There is the autobiography that is implied in the notion of the narrative self and this is common to all human beings. It is an essential part of normal functioning. This, however, is a very different matter to the kind of explicit autobiography that individuals may express. Mixing these two phenomena is a major source of misunderstanding.

Are there fundamentally different types of blobs?

At the beginning of this chapter, I recounted how many anthropologists seem to argue that there are two different kinds of people in the world. What I believe they were talking about was something much less fundamental. They are distinguishing between the people who Strawson call diachronics and those he calls episodics. This is a difference which I rephrase as between these people who have got into the habit of talking about their inner states and those who don't. This is an interesting difference but it does not mean that mankind is divided into two quasi species as is implied in the works I criticise. A surface difference is taken as a difference in substance. What such a mistake leads to is well illustrated by Unni Wikan in her criticism of Geertz's depiction of the Balinese self (Wikan 1990).

If we return to Mauss and Antze and Lambek, we find that they were aware of the distinction between the blob itself and imaginative meta-representations of the blob but, in spite of this, they slide from one topic to the other and in fact only talk of meta-representations when they wish to talk about the blob. Most anthropologists are vaguer and simply talk happily about what meta-representations are as though they *were* the blob.

In those societies where, for historical/cultural reasons, it is acceptable, even encouraged, to talk about internal states of mind, individual motivations and autobiography there are many diachronics and these will often take centre stage. It should be noted, however, that, as they do this, they are not exposing their selves, their individuality, their personhood, their agency, to the harsh light of day. They are doing something quite different; they are using their imagination to tell stories about themselves to others, which should not be mistaken for the complex business of being oneself among others. What they are doing when they are being diachronics, and this is the implicit point of Quinn's criticism of post-modernists, is weaving a narrative using those few aspects of their blob that are easily available to their consciousness, and then re-representing them as a tale *about* themselves, in other words publicly meta-representing themselves. This makes clear the error of the direct 'representational' reading that anthropologists have made of such meta-representational activity, which has led them to consider discourse about the self and others to *be* what it is a representation *of*.

In societies where, in most contexts, such meta-representational talk about one's internal states and motivations is thought inappropriate or even immoral, discourse will obviously not normally be psychologically oriented but will be much more about the rules of behaviour that should be followed in groups, roles, rights and duties and exchange systems. This is my experience among the more remote Malagasy groups I have studied.[2] Such emphasis does not mean we find there an alternative blob, different from the self of the west where the rhetorical emphasis is on individuality and interiority. It is simply that anthropologists, missing their familiar public meta-discourse about the blob, when they are in societies where the glorifying of diachronics does not take place, therefore

---

[2] Though it is important to note also that such talk about internal states can easily be generated as it can in England, thus showing that it exists in some contexts. This I have described in a number of recent publications (Bloch 2005).

concentrate on the discourse about relations and morality, which, in any case, is found in all societies. The anthropologists, quite misleadingly, make this into a compatible, if alternative, blob, a kind of substitute concept of the person, or the individual, or the self or the agent, while in fact it is nothing of the sort. There is thus no basis for a contrast between two types of blob.

This is all the more so as, most likely, we are dealing with a statistical difference, not a categorical one. If the people of modern Britain are, as Strawson argues, divided between phenomenological diachronics and episodics it is likely that the relative proportions are affected by the culture of Britain, not merely by individual dispositions. If that is the case, it is also likely that in other cultures these proportions will be different. In my experience, talk about internal states and individual motivations *does* occur in Malagasy villages, although rarely. The individualist, self-reflexive blob cultures of the west are merely those where many people go in for a lot for diachronic narratives while the 'others' are ones where people are rarely tempted to go in for meta-representation of their internal feelings.[3]

I have used Strawson's distinction between episodics and diachronics to show that anthropology's 'two kinds of people' are nothing of the sort.

---

[3] This is particularly important in making us realise the fundamental difference in the ways we know others and ourselves. We only have empirical access to the blob of others through their explicit discourse and outward behaviour. Although we may, consciously or unconsciously, guess at what might lie below, for most practical purposes we do not need to go beyond outward manifestations for interaction and these are of a different character to being myself and, anyway, greatly simplified. On the other hand, although we may also imagine ourselves as seen through the eyes of others, this will only be a minor part of our blob, most levels of which, as I have argued, are below the level of consciousness.

This difference between knowledge of ourselves and others is important not just theoretically but also methodologically as it is relevant to the way we can use the work of anthropologists in the general enterprise in which I am engaged. Anthropologists inevitably can only study others. They are thus tempted to use the representations we use when dealing with others as though they were simply the 'person' in this or that place.

However, an unfortunate conclusion could be drawn from the above. It might appear at this point that what I have argued is that imaginative meta-representations of the blob are 'cultural' and that the blob itself is 'natural', thereby falling into the old trap. This might be a modification to the theory that some culturalists or universalists might not have too much difficulty in accepting. They could then say: let the different disciplines get on with their own thing, the anthropologists talk about public imaginative meta-representations and the cognitive scientists talk about the fundamental blob. This division of labour would be totally misleading.

Cognitive scientists and social scientists may have been talking of different things with the same words but both really do want to talk about the blob; anthropologists often make clear that they desire to say something about the blob itself but are continually led astray by the easier accessibility of meta-representations. However, if we become aware of what is happening, which is also the source of the tiresome repetition of the debate in the social sciences, then a framework for a proper joint enterprise can be envisaged. This I attempt to approach schematically in the last part of this chapter.

The social blob

First of all, it is important to remember the most significant fact that the levels of the blob I have distinguished are not separate or fully distinct. There is a continuum from the core self to the narrative self (Squire 1992)[4] (see Figure 4). All these levels interact. Thus, the narrative self is continuous with the primate-wide requirements of the minimal self, and the minimal self is continuous with the living-kind-wide requirements of the core self. Similarly, the narrative self is continuous with the minimal self which will itself be affected by the core self. We are psychologically and physically one at all levels.

[4] Squire shows that the old distinction between declarative and non-declarative memory is not neurologically based.

But there is also another aspect to the continuum of the blob. As soon as we are moving to the higher levels, we are also moving from the internal and private level of such factors as the awareness of ownership of one's body and its location towards the public, and therefore inevitably social, expressions of the narrative self.

This gradual move from the private to the public and, above all, its internal continuity, is particularly important if we are to understand how the historical affects the blob. We might be tempted to assume that the private is untouched by the historical process while the public, caught up in social discourse, is entirely cultural. This would be misleading because it would, once again, be to forget the *continuity* of the blob through its various levels. The blob is a process. It is not a matter of a binary contrast but one of more or less. In other words, like icebergs, the blob is 90 per cent submerged but the exposed part has no real independent existence from the submerged part and vice versa.

But to the internal continuity of the blob must be added another continuity: that between blobs. This I have not considered so far and will be a central subject of the next chapter.

Thus, the analogy with icebergs can also mislead because, unlike icebergs, the exposed parts of the different blobs are not fully distinct one from another. They are organically united with each other. We are a social species and, as is the case for other social species, the isolated Cartesian individual cannot be anything other than, what it was for Descartes himself: a thought experiment. It is through the continual complex social exchange between individuals which characterises our species that history/culture becomes part of the process that is the blob. This historical aspect is so because this interchange, in the case of humans, is part of a process which involves not only the interaction of presently living public parts of blobs but also the indirect intercreation of the public parts of living blobs with the once public parts of dead blobs, in some cases public parts of blobs dead long ago.

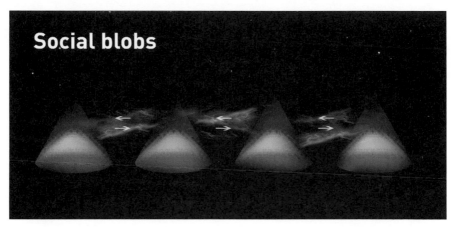

FIGURE 7.

The blob is not just *situated* in this process; it is itself moulded and modified by it to a significant degree. That the social and historical to a certain extent creates the blob has been stressed again and again in both the social science and the cognitive science literature, as it was in the remarks from Mead I quoted above. The social and communicative aspect of humans has meant that the boundary between the individual organism in a species such as our own is only partial in that we go in and out of each others bodies, not only because of the physiological processes of birth and sex but also through the neuro-psychological processes of the synchronisation of minds that occurs in social exchange (Bloch 2007) (see also Humphrey 2007) (see Figure 7).

This process of interpenetration and historical creation is of course what social scientists and especially social and cultural anthropologists have traditionally been emphasising. It will be further explored in the next chapter and it is essential to any theory of the blob. The exposed parts of different blobs are to a varying extent continuous with each other and this is not just at the narrative self levels and therefore at the level of autobiographical memory but also for some aspects of lower levels evoked by the term the 'minimal self', since less explicit but essential forms of joint action and therefore interchange also exist (Knoblich and Sebanz 2008). The merging of public parts of blobs is never complete since differentiation of one's blob from that of others is as necessary for the social process as is the interpenetration of different blobs.

This leads me to my very simple conclusion about the blob. The blob is simultaneously caught up in two quite different continuities, both of which link at either of their poles what are essentially alien elements. One continuum links up and, to a certain extent, merges different but nonetheless distinct blobs, different people linked by social ties, in other words. The other continuum links the totally sub-conscious core blob with the potentially re-represented narrative level. As is the case of the social link, elements that are ultimately different are partially united into a not fully integrated, or integratable, whole.

Thinking of either of these continuities is difficult enough but we have to think of them together! If we do not, the complex phenomenon we have to try to understand drains away with the bath water and we are left with concepts that cannot be related to anything in nature. The error of those cognitive scientists that social scientists such as Durkheim criticised is that they forgot the continuous social historical continuum and thus make the mistakes that most first-year anthropology students have explained to them again and again. We cannot talk of people in general without bearing in mind that they have been and are, to a certain extent, being made different by the social process.

Cognitive scientists have recently discussed extensively the mechanism which makes the cultural nature of humans possible. However, they have not taken on board the obvious implication that because of culture, there are no purely generic humans. The implications of this for research and more particularly cross-cultural research are dramatic: whatever empirical work we want to carry out demands that we first understand our subjects in their unique specificity and not just as fully formed humans who are then superficially affected by culture.

The problem of the social scientists is double. First of all, there is the fact that I discussed already. On the whole, they have only looked at imaginary meta-representations of the blob, though occasionally they do go beyond this to the narrative level in all its forms. The limitation of this perspective is a product of what their research methods makes easily available. They then have either pretended that these levels *were* the total blob or they have argued that these levels were clearly distinct from other levels, thereby implicitly importing the kind of nature/culture dichotomy that, in another register, they often denounce.

Secondly, when thinking about the blob, they have forgotten its internal heterogeneous character and complexity. This is what I have been stressing here. They have forgotten that it seamlessly joins very different types of phenomena, some of which, although inseparable, are totally unaffected by the mechanisms which they study.

Conclusion

I have tried to reconcile the kind of ideas that have characterised anthropological writing on the blob with that which has been produced by cognitive science. I have attempted to build a model which can include in one model the theoretical points and observations that have come from both sides within a system where the different factors that have interested social and cognitive scientists affect different parts of a single natural phenomenon. This is because representations of the human blob have to be compatible with the multiplicity of empirically inseparable processes within which we exist. All living things are caught in two processes: phylogeny and ontogeny.[5] When we are dealing with our species,

---

[5] Our models must, therefore, talk of living things whose specificity, explicitly or implicitly, is comprehensible as the product of the process of natural selection. This is done here in that I have suggested something of the evolutionary history of the blob. These living things must be able to be produced and develop, grow from single cells to the mature phenomena we claim they are. I have not been able

we have to add a third process: that of history. How this interacts with the blob and memory will be considered in different ways in the following chapters. We must keep, at least in the back of our minds, all three processes, otherwise we are forgetting the specific nature of the human animal.

to touch on this here but I have used cognitive science literature which has begun to explore that side of things extensively (e.g. the studies in Moore and Lemmon 2001).

SEVEN

What goes without saying

In chapter 5, I argued that anthropologists often mistakenly identify what are imaginative meta-representations as though these were more basic understandings of time which organise inference and ordinary action. Similarly, in the previous chapter, I argued that anthropologists often mistake imaginative meta-representations of the individual, the self or the person for that knowledge of oneself and others which organises more ordinary and more basic inference and action. Through such misrepresentation, anthropologists are easily led to produce falsely exoticising accounts resulting in such arguments that there are two fundamentally different types of people in the world. These mistakes are indirectly and partly caused by thinking of 'culture' as a self-contained independent system opposed to 'nature'. This is the negative part of the argument. More positively, however, and also in the two previous chapters, I drew attention to elements which are often ignored as a result of the exclusive consideration of these imaginative meta-representations. The reason for these omissions comes in part from the fact that these occasional meta-representations come ready made in explicit and well-formulated language and are thus easily reproducible in ethnographies.

The implicit or the unexpressed is, by definition, much more difficult to reproduce and isolate. What is involved simply cannot be grasped in other ways than in practice and together with other, more fundamental, levels which are constitutive parts of the processes of minds and bodies; processes which are in some cases more or less similar to processes occurring in other primates and even in more remotely related animate beings.

In fact, we are dealing with a range of phenomena which relate to the different levels of the blob distinguished in the previous chapter. As we move down from the narrative self to the core self we are considering types of knowledge which are less and less easily accessible to the consciousness of the actor and also turning towards levels of knowledge which are less and less separable from the processes that produce them. These lower levels are implicit and people find them difficult, or totally impossible, to put into words; yet these are, in many ways, the most important since they are what enables people to operate in the world. For this reason, therefore, they should be central concerns of anthropologists and social scientists generally.

Implicitness is a matter of more or less. Some types of taken-for-granted levels of knowledge can be easily made explicit by people who use them; some require great effort. This gradual and changing degree of implicitness is typical of the nature of human consciousness whose presence is not, as the psychoanalysts would have it, a matter of yes or no.

This chapter examines these different degrees of implicitness. These range from a consideration of knowledge that is taken for granted because it would simply be clumsy and boring to make it explicit, information such as the fact that restaurants are places where one eats, to knowledge and processes of which one is totally unaware. Examples of these would be the knowledge we muster and the mechanisms we set in motion as we produce a word or a sentence or the basic presuppositions concerning causality and temporality that underpin normal reasoning. Yet it would be misleading to distinguish too sharply between these levels of implicitness and process since human beings are continually transforming the totally implicit into the less implicit and perhaps, on occasion, as is the case with Strawson's diachronics, into the explicit and the meta-representational as they construct explicit narratives about themselves. The reverse transformation also occurs easily and frequently such as when the explicit teachings of a driving instructor becomes automatic as one becomes an expert and fluent driver or when we suddenly become aware of the presence of the rules of grammar when we hear someone making a mistake.

This chapter pushes further the examination of what underlies the surface that social and cultural anthropologists observe more easily and argues that only if these implicit or hidden elements which produce the surface are taken into account can we fully understand both the explicit and the implicit which the people we study know. Leach had similarly long ago pointed out the dangers of anthropologists considering explicit statements as the foundation of cognition when he showed that some of the writing reporting strange beliefs concerning conception among Australian Aborigines could just as easily have been made of Christians if one had used the dogma of the virgin birth as evidence that Europeans did not think that a masculine contribution is necessary for a woman to fall pregnant (Leach 1966). In such ways, anthropologists have often mistaken what are understood by the participants to be second-order phenomena, i.e. the constructions which shared imagination and time travel constructs, as the cognitive basis of the knowledge of the world of the people they study. The result of this misapprehension, or perhaps its cause, is that it excuses social scientists from the difficult task of taking into account the implicit which, furthermore, cannot be done without a consideration of mental processes.

This ethnographic problem is merely an epiphenomenon of an even more fundamental error. It comes from not realising that what we can observe from the outside is merely the outward superficial manifestation of the complex activity of the bodies and minds of naturally existing human beings. As social scientists normally can only observe the surface, they are easily tempted to attribute to it a false independent and bounded existence. This leads them to ignore implicit levels which although not on the surface are essential if we are to understand what is going on in front of us. By contrast, the realisation and exposition of this mistake makes clear the dangers involved and how misleading such discounting of the implicit can be. This is what Leach's criticisms of earlier understandings of Australian Aboriginal ideas concerning birth demonstrate so brilliantly. Furthermore, even though this is not so in Leach's case, such demonstration can and should become a first step in reinstating the process of production of the ethnographic surface, especially the psychological process. This ultimately means that the anthropologist has to pay attention to the cognitive. This chapter follows the path of such realisation as it has occurred in the development of anthropological theory. First of all, it looks at criticisms of ethnographic approaches which forget the implicit productive activity that makes actions and speech possible. Then it will look at the ideas of writers who point out the need for doing this. Then it will look at how the work of some cognitive scientists helps us to go yet further in order to reconstruct this process of production of the implicit levels theoretically and who, thereby, enrich our understanding of what social scientists normally observe. Finally, it will examine more closely what the implicit entails and what this means for research methods.

The path towards seeing the ethnographic as the product of active psychological beings

As we saw, the need to take into account implicit processes in order to understand what people do and say is often forgotten in the work of anthropologists. Very often, anthropologists simply avoid having to consider the problem because of a Boasian-like notion which represents what we study as 'culture', that is as an independent self-contained phenomenon. This false realism is the product of the harmful nature/culture dichotomy discussed in previous chapters. The justified insistence on the historical character of human knowledge led the Boasians to view culture as a fully formed independent product, consisting of clear messages transmitted from one individual to another through the course of history. With such a point of view, a complementary consideration of the activity of the minds of the people concerned with producing this knowledge seems unnecessary. This is seen as being on the other side of the divide, as part of 'nature'.

There are, however, a number of theoretical traditions from within the social sciences which can more easily accommodate the implicit and the psychological. These, unlike the mainly American ones considered in chapter 3, have, for the most part, come from Europe and especially from Britain and France. This is because in these countries the subject of anthropology was less captured by the epic confrontation of anthropology with biology which had tempted the cultural anthropologists to ignore the significance of cognitive, social and practical processes. The confrontation was never as intense an issue in Europe and so there was not felt the need to assert quite so militantly the independence of culture as a coherent system of meaning.

In these countries, anthropology significantly adopted the label 'social anthropology' rather than the 'cultural anthropology' of the Americans. Ultimately, of course, the contrast between the social and the cultural is illusory since the 'cultural' requires transmission via social relations and 'social' relations are always affected by the process of history which can be called the 'cultural'. However, the use of the term 'social' stresses more that knowledge exists within the processes of the blob and within the relations of living/acting people interacting amongst themselves rather than within a 'cultural' code.

The origin of 'social anthropology', in Britain at least, is the sociology of Durkheim. This implies a fundamentally different view of meaning to that of the American ideas of the Boas school. Durkheim's main point was that human beings were, above all, social animals and that everything about them had to be understood in that light. As noted in chapter 5, this could lead to an unacceptable relativist view of cognition for the simple reason that, if the bases of cognition were caused by society, and, since there were different types of societies, there must be different types of cognition. Such a position also led Durkheim to deny the precedence of individual and individualist psychology over sociology because, according to him, this would assume that people were the same everywhere, irrespective of social environment, while instead he argued that they were *made* by the type of society in which they lived. It is, however, another aspect of the Durkheimian insistence on the social that I concentrate on in this chapter since this has proved much more fruitful. As could be expected, given the philosophical tradition from which he came, Durkheim was interested in the cognitive bases of the Aristotelian categories but, since he saw these as fundamentally social, this meant that these cognitive foundations existed for him somehow buried in the process of interactions occurring between individuals. The insistence that, once created, cognition was *within* practical life amongst people has had much influence and is particularly relevant here.

The necessity of focussing on the pragmatic aspect of communication for understanding meaning is implied by Durkheim's sociology. The pragmatic is about the relation between message senders and message receivers and about the way language is used and to what ends. This has long been a central concern in linguistics and philosophy. Durkheim's emphasis on the social also implies this. On the other hand, how exactly to describe and analyse something so fleeting and mobile as pragmatic interaction is very difficult. Unlike what has been the case for psychologists, philosophers and linguists, this has not really been a concern of Durkheim or of most social anthropologists. Such omission in social anthropology has created a methodological and theoretical problem that has ever since worried many of the theoreticians who have followed them.

It was Durkheim's disciple Mauss who is often credited as having taken up the challenge frontally. In a number of essays, he stresses how the bodily, the mental and the psychological[1] are simultaneously present in social relations (Mauss 1923–4, 1924, 1935). Mauss sees the implicitness of knowledge as typical of certain types of relations, especially those occurring in the pre-industrial world, where, he argues, all aspects – the bodily, the psychological, the moral and the social – form a totality.

This insistence on unity is further developed by the French sociologist and anthropologist Pierre Bourdieu who claims to have been inspired by Mauss's essay on the body (1935). The three key words he uses in his theoretical discussion are 'practice', 'habitus' and 'embodiment'. The central point which he makes about practice is also influenced by some of Marx's ideas on labour. Bourdieu argues that knowledge is implicit in what people do as they act within the social world rather than in what they say they do or in explicit codes of conduct (Bourdieu 1972). For him, knowledge is thus 'embodied'. That is, it is situated in bodies which have themselves been made by 'habitus'. Habitus is the product of the way people have been brought up and moulded by their society and their culture. Bourdieu is very critical of theories such as those he attributes to Lévi-Strauss and others, which, according to him, look on the social as if from the outside. These make social life appear as if it was governed by a set of rules and abstract master concepts which, according to these theories, are used as a blueprint for life, and which are mistakenly described as though they could remain external to the actions of people involved. According to Bourdieu, such an approach forgets that rules have to be *experienced* as powerful by people. Only then are they able to generate individual action. In other words, whatever has been taken in from the outside as a result of the fact that people are plunged deep in the historical process, which is what Boas would have called the 'cultural', must *appear* as if it was originating from the inside. Internalisation of

---

[1] Mauss tries to maintain the boundaries between psychology and sociology and anthropology as disciplines but his writing, unlike that of Durkheim, goes all the other way.

the external then makes it appear as straightforward for the actor since her body has been 'habituated' by the habits and context within which the person has grown up and lives. This, nonetheless, largely remains implicit and this is what Bourdieu calls 'habitus'.

The approach to meaning developed by Bourdieu, as well as that of his followers, whether conscious or otherwise, such as Giddens (1981), Ingold (2000) and Munn (1986), is extremely fruitful. I retain from it that we must always remember that whatever we do and say or can observe in others is the product of internal processes. As such, these approaches are a fundamental criticism of the semiological or hermeneutic tack of writers such as Lévi-Strauss and Geertz. The difference between the two approaches is very significant for understanding modern anthropology since, explicitly or implicitly, the Boasian cultural approach has dominated in a variety of forms and still does even though many of its practitioners believe they have freed themselves from it. There are, however, also problems with these so-called 'practice' approaches, many of which have already been discussed by Strauss and Quinn in the second chapter of their book (1997 ch. 2).

At first sight, these appear mainly to be matters of imprecision, perhaps simply due to the difficulty of capturing ethnographically the fleeting knowledge which informs action as it occurs. The insistence on the implicit which is not normally separated from the flow of life means that it is, almost by definition, extremely difficult to pin down and study. This is so both for the theoretician and the ethnographer. However, there often lies behind this difficulty a quite unnecessary limitation in the tools that could be used to overcome it. These practice theories are all cognitive theories: they are about learning and the storing of information, yet they avoid making the effort of trying to understand mental and psychological processes seriously. As a result, the cognitive claims made remain totally vague and even circular.

The term 'habitus', used by Bourdieu, illustrates the vagueness which hinders analysis. Its Latinate form barely hides the fact that it does not mean much more than what habit produces. The word 'embodiment' is even vaguer. It is not clear whether it is meant metaphorically or literally. This imprecision is not, however, ultimately due to the ethnographic difficulty of documentation and interpretation; it comes from a basic theoretical muddle. At first, what the use of the word seems to seek to do is describe what the participants in social life feel in social situations. Thus, a Berber man may well declare and experience a feeling of disgust towards an abhorrent practice and say that it 'makes him sick in the pit of his stomach'. This feeling, which may well be a direct quotation of the words used by actors, creeps into the texts of the writers discussed here where it appears as the *cause* of the actions that are performed. Embodiment thus becomes an *explanation* of motivation and what produces action. A feeling in the stomach may well be the type of account that the participants would recognise as appropriate. Thus, in this limited way the practice/embodied approach is a valid account of *post hoc* explanations that may be given by those concerned. However, it is hardly a useful account of the history that has meant that a Berber man feels in this way when, for example, someone makes a pass at his sister. More significantly, for the subject of this book, it is not an account of what is going on in the stomach, or any other part of the body, far less in the brain, of the person who makes such a statement. Such explicit formulations are interesting and should be reflected upon, but, in the end, we cannot escape the fact that we do not think with our stomach and that the physiological manifestations of emotions are not simply localised in the abdomen. These are caused by the working of our nervous system, especially in its central mechanism, the brain. The phenomenological account of Bourdieu may be a good paraphrase of what the actors say but it cannot become what it pretends to be, that is an exploration of the roots of action.

The basis of the problem is simply that we as human beings, just like other animals, are not conscious of the mechanisms which bring about our doing what we do or saying what we say, or of the knowledge which we mobilise as we perform actions. This is so, and as we shall see below, it has to be so, if only because of the speed and necessary fluency with which we normally act and speak. If we ignore the difficult fact that the causes of our actions and speech are not available to us but require to be grasped through considerations which are external to consciousness, we mistakenly seek to discover them in the actions and the words themselves. This creates the mistake which was discussed in the chapter on time and more particularly in the discussion of *The Fame of Gawa*. There, Munn argues that the fundamental understanding of time and space is created in the flow of the occurrence of speech and action which she, as an ethnographer, can observe while instead these categories have to be already present since they are what enables the production of acts and words. To understand this, it is necessary to break out of the practice itself in order to see how it has come about. This is why social scientists cannot limit themselves to the traditional resources of their discipline. They will need to benefit from what neurologists and psychologists can tell them about learning, the storage of familiar information, memory and the relation of emotion and cognition. By stressing the need to understand individual motivation and the processes that lead to action in living people, Bourdieu takes us to a point where we cannot do without the work of cognitive scientists, but he himself seems unwilling to take the further necessary step.

Before considering what such further steps involve, it is necessary to discuss the work of another theorist who had reached Bourdieu's conclusions half a century before but who, in many ways, had taken us further forward. This is the Polish/British anthropologist Malinowski. Malinowski's theoretical position was always phrased as simply deriving from his method of research which he called 'participant observation' (Malinowski 1922). Malinowski was reacting against the way anthropology had been done before him when ethnographic data was obtained either second hand, either from the writings of missionaries and travellers, or first hand, but through interview methods. An example of the type of field work Malinowski was criticising was that carried out by Seligman who was Malinowski's predecessor and patron at the London School of Economics where both taught. Seligman had been an indefatigable field worker who had obtained a great mass of information by interviewing 'natives' in the British colonies in Africa, South Asia and Australasia. The way this field work was carried out was for Seligman to arrange with the colonial authorities for meetings with influential local persons. By contrast, Malinowski argued that the culture of those studied could only be grasped 'in the context of situation' within which it was produced. This meant that the anthropologist had to be there when things happened and had therefore to understand the local language in order to grasp knowledge as it was used within practice and within the flow of action and social relations. The ethnographer thus had to *participate* in the lives of those he studied for very long periods. This was necessary because *post hoc* recounting was always misleading. Asking informants to create narratives and stories about themselves and their actions, as was required in Seligman-like interviews, would, however sincere the informants, falsify the lived embodied reality of knowledge in practice. It is inevitably impossible for the practitioners to put effectively into words the process of their lives, not only because their business is to live them rather than describe them, but more significantly because their actions and words rest on presuppositions which are not the subject of discourse and of which the actors are not conscious. Revealingly, Malinowski uses the word which is usually attributed to Bourdieu – 'embodiment' – to explain the difference between what people retrospectively say they do and the experience of doing it (Malinowski 1922: ch. 1).

Through such arguments, Malinowski transformed what at first was simply a method for data gathering into a theory of meaning in practice. According to him, the reason why the anthropologist had to do participant observation was not simply because this was a good way of obtaining data but because the data itself existed only in the practical production of actions created by people interacting among themselves. If the anthropologist did not do the kind of field work he advocated, Malinowski would necessarily misrepresent what it was that was being studied because he would separate meaning from people involved in and producing meaning. It is not surprising therefore that nowhere did Malinowski develop the implications of his theoretical position better than in his work on language. Nowhere is it clearer just how far reaching are the implications of the difference between the cultural anthropology of the Boasian tradition and the social anthropology of Malinowski. For this reason, in the following section and in order to advance the general argument, I focus on what the different anthropological theories we have looked at in this chapter suggest or state about language. This is a useful way to reveal just how fundamental is the difference between, on the one hand, such as Bourdieu or Malinowski and, on the other hand, the Boasians and their heirs. Furthermore, it shows why the cognitive perspective must enrich that of the Malinowski–Bourdieu approach.

The semiotic tradition

The Boasian idea of culture has always represented culture as being very language-like. This is especially the case in the form it was to take in the work of his pupils. Culture for the Boasians is an integrated system of meanings which enables people to deal with the world by classifying it according to their own, culturally inherited, unique way of seeing things. For them, language and culture cut up reality into categories and it is only once these systems are established in the mind of the participants that people are able to act coherently. As was discussed in chapter 3, in their enthusiasm in combating reductionist biologisms, the Boasians came to stress culture as an independent coherent system even as independent of actors and social relations. This was, in the words of Boas's one-time follower Kroeber, 'super organic'. Culture preceded action, rather like the rules of football must precede a match for the event to be at all possible. This theory had two implications.

First, it followed from the view of culture as 'super-organic' that there is no clear place for taking into account constraints coming from the environment. For the Boasians, there is no need to consider the complex relations that might exist between the 'world as it exists in movement' and mental processes. Things in the world cannot challenge or interfere with culture since the world can only be known via culture. There was thus no justification on pragmatic grounds for being suspicious of reports that Australian Aborigines deny the importance of sex for procreation, or that this or that group of people have a 'cyclical' view of time simply because of the evident lack of fit of such representations with practical life.

Secondly, such a view of culture leads easily to the assumption that culture forms a coherent system, all at one level. This follows from the idea that it is a kind of structured encyclopaedia. Culture is imagined as a kind of absolute all-embracing unavoidable lens placed between people and the world. In such a view, meanings define each other through their interrelations much as the idea of parent implies that of child. Culture is therefore 'patterned' and patterning.

Because such a view of culture implies that 'culture' is a taxonomic tool which organises whatever is out there, it has a natural affinity with the common idea that language similarly determines what we know. Such an approach easily leads to culture being understood in a quasi-linguistic way. The proposition that culture is a kind of language has taken many forms. At it simplest, it consists in the idea that our perception of the world is determined by the classifications implicit in our lexicon. Arguing in this way, we could say that the word 'animal' corresponds to the concept 'animal' which groups together certain species such as rabbits, lions and mice but excludes others such as daisies or moulds. In such a view, the vocabulary of culture creates the parameters of thought.

An extreme form of this type of thinking was the Sapir–Whorf hypothesis which was touched on in chapter 5. Another version of this is found in the work of a group of 1960s American anthropologists, who, although they called themselves 'cognitive anthropologists' (Tyler 1969), paid no real attention to psychological or neurological factors since they assumed these were regulated by the vocabulary. They used a method called componential analysis which involved cross indexing related terms to discover the minimal lexical items which they contained. This method amounted to examining the principles of the vocabulary in order to discover within it the principles of organisation of the world view of the people who spoke the local languages. As such, this method implicitly accepted the Whorfian notion of equivalence between thought and language[2] and thus avoided the questions concerning that relation which will be considered in what follows. With views such as these, trying to understand cognition by going beyond or below what people explicitly say makes no sense since what they say forms the framework of what they think. Furthermore, such authors would argue that examining discourse critically by placing words in the context of what we know about the world, as Leach suggests we should in the case of statements about the virgin birth, is dangerous. It misleads, since so doing would inevitably involve using our own view, which the Whorfians or the componential analysts believe is buried in our vocabulary, while the people discussed would see things in their different but equally valid way, simply because they use a different vocabulary. Yet a further example of this way of thinking is found in the work of two kinship theorists already mentioned, Needham and Schneider. Although they thought of themselves as very different, they both criticised their predecessors in the subject by arguing that because they had attempted to translate kinship words from an exotic language into English they had misrepresented the thought of the people studied since, implicitly for Needham and Schneider, words organise cognition and can only be defined within the framework of a

---

[2] For an early critique of the misleading psychological implications of this method, see Wallace 1965.

total vocabulary (Needham 1971; Schneider 1984). According to them, doing such direct translation inevitably misleads. It is what anthropologists love to denounce as 'ethnocentrism': that is illegitimately imputing our way of seeing things on to others of a different culture/language. Interestingly, this example shows well how the use of the equation 'words equal thought' easily leads to a denial of the very possibility of a comparative, and therefore of a general, theoretical anthropology. This is because, since the semantic field of words in different languages never correspond exactly, there remains little to be said in general about human cognition other than that things are different in different places.

There are also less straightforward linguistic ways of understanding culture that nonetheless seem to follow a similar logic. Thus, Lévi-Strauss adapted from the linguist Saussure the idea that culture consists of a large number of signs which stand for concepts; in the same manner in this type of theory the sound of a word stands for a concept. For example, the word 'tree' stands for the mental concept *tree*. This type of scheme is often called 'semiotics'. Again, Geertz in a somewhat similar way sees culture as a system of public symbols which, although he does not equate them with words, do, in fact, seem to be super mental concepts straightforwardly indicated by words. Thus, according to Geertz, people 'read' the world by using these signifying symbols/words.

For all these writers, culture is therefore a coherent arbitrary code of signifiers, the product of the vagaries of history, which form a determining filter between the world and the individual's senses and desires. From such a perspective, culture exists at one level only because it is a scheme independent of the actions of the people who use it to communicate with each other and who operate in the world in which these communications take place. With this view of culture, ethnography rapidly becomes a matter of describing the culture/language filter and its structure in order to make it emerge for the reader of ethnography so that she can, somehow, escape ethnocentrism and use it to understand exotic cultures. This kind of theoretical position has never stopped recurring, most recently in the work of ethnographers who talk of the different 'ontologies' of people.

There are writers in the Boasian tradition, and a number of related ones, who argue for a rarely fully analysed equation between words and 'classifiers', 'world views', 'concepts', 'symbols' and 'ontologies'. These word/concepts form systems which organise the way the world is apprehended. They are seen as signifiers of parts of the external world; however, they do this independently from what they signify, rather like a telephone directory, which gives the numbers of the subscribers, without being in anyway part of them. With this point of view, the task of the ethnographer is to be a writer of a kind of bilingual dictionary of words, or symbols, or concepts, since according to this type of theory these are assumed to be much the same kind of thing. With an ethnography/dictionary the reader can see what the exotic word/concepts refer to and compare them with his own system of meaning. To produce such an ethnography/dictionary it is clear that the ethnographer does not need to get too involved in the normal practice of the people studied where these signifier systems are used since she only needs to establish context-free meanings. She can stand back and forget about cognitive processes.

The pragmatic approach

This type of semiology is exactly what Malinowski and Bourdieu reject when they insist that meaning can only exist in practice. For authors like them, and unlike Boasians, Geertz or Lévi-Strauss, the signifier is never separate from what it signifies or of its use. This fundamental difference between the two approaches becomes particularly clear when we contrast the theories of language of some Boasians and those of Malinowski himself.

Strangely, Malinowski's extraordinarily bold ideas on meaning were developed by him as though they applied only to 'primitive' languages though he was in fact, developing a fundamental theory of meaning that applies to language in general.[3] However, in what follows, I assume that, unbeknown to him, he was developing a *general* theory of language.

Malinowski's theory of language was first outlined within the context of his study of the agricultural practices of the Trobriand islanders (Malinowski 1935). What he was ostensibly trying to study was how people co-operated in shared agricultural tasks. These involved social relations based on the flow of communication occurring between the co-operators as they were also engaging in non-verbal physical activities. These activities were not merely social but also involved organic relationships with plants and the soil. In the cases he examined, the significant tasks were activities such as planting crops, weeding, etc. The necessary communication for co-ordinating the work involved the use of language, but Malinowski argued, such use of language could not be separated from the other aspects of the activities. With such a point of view, the traditional approach to signification which is implicit in Whorf, the componential analysts and Geertz and their followers is unacceptable precisely because it does not consider communication as a practical/social activity. These approaches visualise language as a system for representations of something which is external to what is represented. For example, saying that the cat is on the mat is understood as simply a way of telling others that the cat is indeed on the mat, but the production of the sounds is considered separable from the reasons why anybody might want to say such a thing, to whom and for what purpose. By contrast, for Malinowski, the meaning of the words cannot be grasped unless these

---

[3] Intriguingly, Mauss did the same, arguing that his innovative and very general theory of the totality of action only applied to primitive societies.

other aspects are also taken into account. For him, saying something is always an action which is part of a system of intentions and social relations. For him, there are many uses for language other than description. The meaning of speech acts cannot be understood unless the latter are put within the context of these many different uses and ultimately within the context of the whole social process. In this way, Malinowski convincingly argues that it would be ridiculous to see the speech acts of the Trobrianders in their gardens as merely a matter of people telling each other things about the external world, as in a lecture about various agricultural activities to a captive student audience. The meaning of what is said during gardening cannot be separated from the task of co-ordinating agricultural activities in agricultural contexts by means of language and through other means.

It has been noted by a number of writers (e.g. Rose 1980) how similar Malinowski's ideas about meaning and language are to those that the philosopher Wittgenstein developed towards the end of his life in the book published as *Philosophical Investigations* (Wittgenstein 1953). There, Wittgenstein rejected what he called the picture theory of meaning which considers language as a simple matter of creating pictures, in other words, considering that speaking is a matter of informing listeners of a state of affairs as, for example, that the cat is on the mat but for the benefit of unspecified people in unspecified places. According to Wittgenstein, this picture view underlies much of philosophy, but we may note that it is also the view of meaning implicit in the theories of the Boasians, Lévi-Strauss, Geertz and many other anthropologists. By contrast, Wittgenstein insisted that language should first of all be seen as 'a form of action'. One should not ask what a word means or stands for but rather what can be done with it. In arguing in this way, Wittgenstein is very similar to Malinowski though the work of the former has been much more developed by a large number of other philosophers such as Austin in his book *How to Do Things with Words* (1962) and Searle in his book on *Speech Acts* (1969). Malinowski the linguist, on the other hand, has had few followers.[4] Even those scholars who are close to anthropology and whose views are close to his tend to forget Malinowski and to trace their intellectual genealogy back to Wittgenstein and other philosophers such as Austin. Thus linguists such as Grice (1968), Levinson (1983) and Sperber and Wilson (1986), who like Malinowski concentrate on the social relations between speakers and hearers, hardly ever mention him.

The similarity between Malinowski and the later Wittgenstein has been noted by a few authors (Langoenden 1968; Gellner 1998) but it is also very instructive to consider the difference between Wittgenstein and the other philosophers, on the one hand, and Malinowski, on the other. Wittgenstein's concern with language is above all motivated by a critique of older philosophical positions, including his own. He calls for the placing of the study of language within practical and social life but he himself never really does this. After all, he and his followers were philosophers and not anthropologists. When he or Austin or Searle or Grice want to show how language is used in practice, they invoke little imaginary scenarios or thought experiments, not situations which actually occurred or might occur. Furthermore, they really only focus on the language aspect of these imaginary scenarios thereby implicitly negating the significance of the aspects they stress should be taken into account. This is because these other aspects are not linguistic matters but practical activities, movements and engagements with the world. Malinowski's trajectory is the opposite. He starts from his study of actual occurring events, for example what goes on as the Trobrianders cultivate their gardens or when they recite spells over their canoes before they set out on dangerous Kula journeys, and *then* considers the place of language within the material and social process. There is a way one could say that by the time Wittgenstein was writing *Philosophical Investigations* he had got himself into a position where he should have given up philosophy and

[4] With a few notable exeptions such as J. R. Firth and Langoenden.

should have instead become an anthropologist. Malinowski, of course, was one already.

The cognitive contribution: concepts

This discussion of language and more particularly of words shows well the significance for social science of the pragmatic approach. It also allows us to focus on how such an approach can help us in understanding the old philosophical and anthropological problem of the relationship of words to the actions involved in their use and the relationship of words to concepts. For this, however, we need whatever help work by cognitive scientists can supply since the pragmatic approach focuses on the thinking and acting person rather than on disembodied messages seemingly unconnected with the mind of those who have produced them. However, it is striking how rarely social scientists have sought this help.

Concepts are the basic element of thought, and anthropologists such as the Boasians quite rightly stressed that their origin is to be partly explained as the product of a unique and specific history. However, as we have seen, stressing this fact to the exclusion of all other considerations has finally led to a complete misrepresentation of what is involved in the study of the working of the social process. Much more than their cultural origin needs to be taken into account.

In order to approach the question of the place of concepts, the first task is one of ground clearing, and this requires distinguishing concepts from words. Anthropologists often write about concepts but rarely make use of the work of cognitive scientists. An example is the subtle and full discussion of *ur* given to us in the book *Fluid Signs* (1984), by Valentine Daniel, concerning the Tamils of South India. The richness of the ethnography gives us a chance to explore the issues raised in this chapter and he also offers a discussion of these same issues in his introduction. His approach, however, is very different from what is argued for here and in this way it offers the opportunity to examine the semiological theories he uses. *Ur* is a Tamil word which clearly has great importance for those who use it. It indicates a galaxy of ideas concerning the way people belong to a significant locality. Valentine Daniel explains that the word can be used in a number of ways varying from highly charged ones to simple matters of giving directions. Because of this, 'defining' the significance of the word *ur* seems very difficult. Valentine Daniel acquaints us with the problem in his introduction on the place of meaning in people's lives. He draws on ideas from various authors, mainly American, who have struggled with these kinds of problems. These authors include anthropologists such as Geertz, Schneider and Sahlins and philosophers, especially Pierce, who had developed a form of semiotics which he had labelled semeiotics. Perhaps because of the multiplicity of his guides a term such as *ur* gets called all sorts of things by Valentine Daniels: word, concept, symbol, sign, etc. As a result, we are rapidly and inevitably sucked into a caricatural academic definitional discussion. When we turn to the ethnography, however, things become much clearer. What Valentine Daniel is observing are the uses of the word and, on that basis and other things he knows about Tamil society, he tries to locate *ur* in Tamil thought. The slippage from word to thought processes is clear. He tries to locate a concept, somehow related to the use of the word *ur*. Putting matters thus may not, at first, appear very different from the way Valentine Daniel, and most other anthropologists, would do. However, instead of mixing up two very different types of phenomena, I want to emphasise the difference.

Concepts are mental phenomena and so we must 'look inside the head to account for the productivity of thought, for how concepts can fit together to form thoughts' (Carey 2009: p. 514). To this, I would add that we must simultaneously look at the social and practical process within which concepts are activated and used, a process which includes, but is not reduced to, the production and understanding of language and other forms of communication. As Malinowski rightly stressed, we engage in the task only superficially if we do not make the effort to understand the co-occurrence of the mental process and the social process. Both are necessary. Not to include a consideration of the mental is like studying the movements of a car while forgetting about the driver. Forgetting about the social is like forgetting that it is a car which is being driven.

Concepts are items of knowledge stored in the mind; they are elements of thought. Because they are mental features, there is nothing strange in the fact that there are many concepts for which no word can be used to indicate them. That this is possible is made evident when we bear in mind that pre-linguistic infants already have concepts (Waxman and Booth 2003). The same is also true of the congenitally deaf and dumb. But, even people who possess language often use concepts for which no words can be used. The linguist Fillmore gives the example of the blue light that policemen sometimes place on the roof of their cars. Most people do not know what these are called though they do know that, when they see one, they have to be particularly careful not to be speeding (Fillmore 1971).

Because concepts are totally different kinds of things to words, the presence of the implicit and the unspoken in social practice is not surprising while, of course, it would be difficult to imagine concept-less speech.[5] The fact that concepts are not the same type of phenomena as language is a key argument in favour of Malinowskian field work since he shows how the concepts of the Trobrianders can only be studied by imagining the mind of the participants as they go about their practical activities and not directly from what they say. Most concepts are probably linked to words but this does not mean the word and the concept are identical. Indeed, an interesting dialectic exists between words and concepts. This has been much studied, especially in child development as the infant learns to speak (Waxman and Booth 2003). A great deal of

---

[5] A mental handicap called Williams syndrome does seem to involve the use of words unrelated to concepts.

research has discussed how previously unnamed concepts, for example concerning familiar objects, are affected and modified when the child learns a word that can point towards a preformed concept (Bowerman and Choi 2003). Thus, as our understanding of concepts has progressed, our conception of them has become less and less directly wordlike; this, paradoxically, has enabled us to study the relation between these two very different phenomena.

The older theory of concepts, usually called the classical theory, represented concepts as tools for classifying the world. This type of approach was clearly inspired by the way dictionaries define the proper usage of a word and it is also implied by the semiotic approach discussed above. There, concepts are explained in terms of necessary and sufficient features that justify inclusion or exclusion of a phenomenon. These can then be said to 'belong' to a particular concept. According to such a theory, a competent speaker of English decides that the flying animal in front of her is a bird by mentally ticking off the necessary features for inclusion, features such as: a beak, the ability to fly, feathers and so on. Such a view of concepts, therefore, implies a notion of culture as a massive system of classification which forms a grid for cognition. By implication, it defines the task of the ethnographer as reproducing the dictionary-like entries which concepts have created in the mind of the people studied. We have already come across such a view. It is implied in the work of anthropologists such as Lévi-Strauss, the Boasians and Geertz. This cultural grid would consist of the list of necessary and sufficient features which explains why a particular phenomenon is grouped with others as cases of the 'concept' and why it is distinguished and contrasted from other phenomena with which it should not be grouped. Like so many others in the Boasian tradition, the American anthropologist Lounsbury was quite explicit about this (Lounsbury 1964). According to him, the person learns the cultural or vocabulary grid and then she sees the world via the grid and can then, inevitably, only act upon it in terms of the grid's logic. This kind of idea lies at the back of much traditional anthropology. For example, the reason why anthropologists who studied kinship from Morgan on paid so much attention to kinship terms was that they saw kinship terminology as the grid by which an individual classifies her kinsmen in terms of concepts defined by necessary and sufficient characteristics. Since these writers assumed, perhaps rightly, that ancient societies were only organised by kinship, this meant that for them the pattern formed by kinship terms was a quick guide to the way these societies were organised.

The notion of 'culture' as a system of classification organised by concepts which are defined in terms of necessary and sufficient characteristics came under challenge in the 1970s through the work of the psychologist Eleanor Rosch. She was able to demonstrate that American speakers of English had in their minds a concept of what birds were which did not correspond at all to the way the word 'bird' would be defined in a dictionary. The mental concept is only vaguely indicated by the word bird. It is focussed on a typical, or a prototypical bird. The concept has no sharp edges as would be implicit in the way words are defined by necessary and sufficient features. In the case studied by Rosch, the prototype, or the focus, is a bird that corresponds to the robin. She demonstrated this by showing that speakers of English took more or less time to decide whether the image they were shown on a screen was a bird depending on whether it was *more or less* like a robin. Furthermore, animals that were called birds by English speakers but which clearly departed from the prototype, for example penguins and ostriches, did so each in very different ways. She concluded that the concept *in the mind* did not form a clearly bounded coherent category. Such concepts as those indicated by the word bird are not a matter of either/or, as is implied in the classical theory of concepts, or as would be implied by their assimilation to words in the semiological theories of culture. They are a matter of differential types of closeness to a prototype (Rosch 1973; Rosch and Mervis 1975). It is this type of fuzzy concepts that people live by and which organises their inferences and not the words which can be given much more precise though much less rich definition when lexicographers go about their business.

Since the pioneering work of Rosch, a great deal of discussion and empirical work has taken place concerning the nature of the core of concepts which Rosch had called 'prototype'. Recently, some authors have argued that the core is less abstract than is sometimes suggested by the word prototype but that it is more a matter of a known case, a best example, against which other examples are compared in terms of more or less and in a variety of ways (Medin and Schaffer 1978). By contrast with the best example theory, a number of other recent authors have argued that the core is composed of a kind of knot of theories which are used to guide the individual in her varied inferences. These theories are best thought of as guides for deciding such things as whether to call a particular animal a bird or how to behave towards it. This view of concepts is often called 'theory theory' (Murphy and Medin 1985; Carey 1991). It suggests a much more active view of conceptual thought than the classical theory or even the prototype theory. According to such a theory of concepts, the concept bird may contain at its core such theories as that birds fly, that they lay eggs, that they are eatable and so on. With such an understanding of the core of the concept a first encounter with a bat may initiate an internal debate about what to do with the animal, what word to use, etc.

The existence of such active internal mental 'debate' is particularly interesting for anthropologists. A possibility which seems to follow naturally from understanding the core of concepts as a knot of theories is that the debate it implies can be continuous with a debate *between* people engaged in a social exchange of inferences. In such a case, the internal thought process or debate is not sharply distinct from the social cultural process of exchange. This also means that modifications initiated in the external debate can modify the internal debate and vice versa.

Conceptual knowledge is not, however, quite as much in a state of flux as theories such as theory theory might, at first, suggest. This is so for two very different reasons. The first is that among the implicit theories of theory theory many are derived from core knowledge, and are probably based on innate predispositions such as the implicit theory of duration which was discussed in the chapter on time. These give an *a priori* grounding to the internal and external inferential process. For example it is quite likely that concepts concerning kinship contain a sub-conscious non-negotiable core of meaning which becomes an element in the various representations that the historical process creates (Bloch and Sperber 2002).

A second reason, which need not necessarily be distinct from the first, is that many concepts seem to be represented in the mind as having an essence. This has been again and again demonstrated for natural kinds. The latter are phenomena which are thought of as given and not negotiable by contrast with the products of human activity which means that natural kinds are experienced as immutable in their core and beyond human circumstances (Atran 1990). Inferences about them are in terms of such an implicit essence which always transcends any characteristic that may be expressed. The essence is experienced as being ultimately unknowable (Medin and Ortony 1989). This feeling of the *a priori* character of the essence is well revealed in an experiment in which subjects declared that a racoon which had been totally transformed so that every part of it has been made to be totally like that of a skunk was still *essentially* a racoon (Keil 1989: ch. 11). Thus, essentialised concepts not only imply much implicit content but also this implicit content remains totally inaccessible to the consciousness of those whose minds operate with them.

The significance of these developments in our understanding of the nature and the organisation of concepts in the mind are particularly important for the social sciences where concepts are so often equated with words. This can be illustrated by an article by J. Parry about the ethnography of India (Parry 1991). Parry was intervening in a contro-versy among Indianist anthropologists concerning the relation of two

Hindi words, one of which can be translated as 'pollution' and the other as 'inauspiciousness'. The various contributors to the debate were disagreeing about the relationship and the differences between the two words which they often called 'concepts'. In the course of the argument, these scholars were coming up with different and often contradictory lists of features for defining the two words/concepts. Parry's intervention consisted in pointing out that treating this issue as though it was a matter of defining words was misleading. At issue were the mental concepts that the words were pointing towards when spoken. Then, relying on prototype theory, Parry explains that, most probably, the two concepts had uncertain and varied extensions, although they probably had clearer cores. The extensions might well overlap. The core for the concept which was indicated by uses of the word for inauspiciousness might well have been a widow. The prototype for pollution might have been animal faeces. This, however, could only have been demonstrated with the kind of experimental work done by Rosch. Varied phenomena were probably more or less associated with widows and faeces in a variety of ways. Some may well have been associated with both. Viewed in this light, the kind of lexicographic turn the debate had taken was simply irrelevant and misleading for understanding mental phenomena such as the concepts of the people studied.

It is interesting that Wittgenstein had already argued something similar to prototype theory when discussing the word 'games', though, in fact, what he was arguing seems to be about the concept of games rather than about the word (Wittgenstein 1953). If we understand him in this way, we find that he had arrived at a very similar conclusion to that of Rosch. For him, it was pointless to try to define 'games' in terms of necessary and sufficient characteristics. Such an attempt could never include such varied activities as a child playing with a doll, a game of football and gambling in a casino. It was only that these things had 'family resemblances'. That was all that could be said of the semantic field of the concept. This view fits in well with a general approach to meaning as part of practice which he also initiated since what words are chosen is a by-product of the activity of minds engaged in what Malinowski calls 'the context of situation' or what Bourdieu calls 'practice' and not of the kind of definition that would be given in a dictionary.

The significance for anthropology of the essentialism of certain concepts is also great. Whether only natural kind concepts are thought of in an essentialist way or whether many more concepts are conceptualised as having an essence is a matter of debate. What is important, however, are the implications of essentialism for inferential and social processes. An example of such possible significance is revealed in a study of the concept of slavery found in modern highland Madagascar. Slavery was abolished in Madagascar in 1896. In certain parts of the island the descendants of slaves are empirically indistinguishable from the descendants of free people, especially since individuals from both groups are often equally well off. Yet descendants of freemen still refuse to intermarry with descendants of slaves. When Malagasy of free descent are asked for the reason for this taboo they are unsure. If pushed, they come up with a variety of *ad hoc* and unconvincing explanations. What they are sure about, however, is that the taint of slavery remains even though they cannot exactly capture in words what it is. They use the concept of slavery assuming it is organised around an implicit yet hidden essence which only manifests itself in a shadowy form in the actions of people guided by minds influenced by it (Regnier forthcoming).

The various theories of concepts reviewed here apply better to some concepts than others. Some concepts, such as odd numbers, for example, can be accounted for quite well by the classical theory; other concepts, such as that which is pointed to by the Hindi words for inauspiciousness and pollution, are best thought of in terms of prototype theories. Concepts such as those indicated in English by the word 'bird' are illuminated by theory theory. Understanding still others, such as 'slavery' in Madagascar, require a consideration of essentialism.

It is also clear that concepts can change their semantic character during development without the verbal referent reflecting this change, thus showing once again how the two kinds of phenomena must be kept apart. The psychologist Frank Keil has studied the concepts that are pointed to by the word 'uncle' in English (1989). The experimental tasks set by Keil show that for younger children the concept is best understood in prototype or 'best exemplar' terms. For these younger children, it could be paraphrased as 'an uncle is someone who resembles, in one way or another, people who, like my uncle, have a moustache and smoke a pipe'. However, the concept indicated by the same word for adults is more like a classical concept which could be rendered as 'an uncle is, first of all, a male who is a sibling of my parents or a spouse of a sibling of my parents'. There is a good deal of evidence to suggest that such gradual transformation of concepts from prototype to classical to theory theory goes on continually throughout maturation and even during adulthood as people learn about new things while the words they use stay the same.

The example of the concept indicated by the word 'uncle' used by Keil is particularly interesting for anthropologists given the importance that kinship and kinship terms have had for the discipline. Distinguishing concepts from words and bearing in mind the variety of mental processes that words may relate to completely changes the significance that can be attributed to their uses in different situations by different people. It totally changes the kind of thing indicated by the phrase 'kinship system'.

Thus, the knowledge which informs what people say and do cannot be accessed directly. The external observable phenomenon must be understood as merely the outward partial product of much more complex processes of production. These processes of production therefore need to be reconstructed in theoretical imagination and this can only be done in part through a reflection on the different character and inferential potential of concepts as part of the practical production of thought and action. In a way, this is what Malinowski, Wittgenstein and Bourdieu insisted on. However, because they did not push their criticisms of other theories to a stage where they would move to a more positive understanding of the cognitive processes to which they were pointing, they left the job half done. For this, they needed the help of the different cognitive sciences.

Scripts, schema, mental models, cultural models

A number of psychologists and anthropologists have used a variety of terms to talk about what are, in fact, large concepts. These have variously been called scripts (Schank and Abelson 1977), schemas (Bartlett 1932), mental models (Johnson-Laird 1983; Bloch 1992) and cultural models (D'Andrade 1995; Strauss and Quinn 1997). What is indicated by these terms is particularly interesting for anthropology and the social sciences in general. A consideration of what is involved shows well the need to take into account psychological processes for understanding what anthropologists seek to capture.

The notion indicated by these words was first discussed by Schank and Abelson (1977) and is well illustrated by the example they used. This concerns the concepts surrounding the phenomenon indicated by the word 'restaurant'. This example concerns a story about two people who are having a rather anxious dinner party in a restaurant. The point that Schank and Abelson make is that nowhere in the story are we told that restaurants are places where you eat food, where you have to pay for it, where there are chairs, etc. All this is taken for granted, or rather inferred, by both speaker and hearer of the story. In other words, for the story to be understood, a great deal more information than the story contains explicitly needs to be known, and to be known to be known, by both speaker and hearer. Such massive implicit knowledge is necessary not only for understanding a narrative; it is also necessary for action, especially joint action. It is not difficult to imagine someone walking into a restaurant and being efficiently shown to their table by a waiter with only the minimal verbal exchange. This is possible because the waiter can assume that the customer knows what goes on in restaurants in general and the client can assume that the waiter knows that he will know what to expect in general in a restaurant. Furthermore, all will probably know what kind of restaurant is involved. Most probably, the client will have taken in a number of small but diagnostic signs. These may include linguistic indications such as the fact that somewhere on the building is actually written 'restaurant' but also much less explicit signs such as the type of curtains he can glimpse and the quality of the material of which they are made. Once again, observable actions and words need to be understood as mere occasional surface phenomena of quite different underlying processes.

This is particularly significant for social scientists. It shows how very little perceived stimulus, via the activation of schemas, can supply a mass of implicit information. This was well demonstrated by Holland and Quinn. They show how, simply by being told of an advertisement for beer in which lumberjacks are present we are able to obtain a pretty good idea how the people in the scene are dressed and what kind of beer is involved (1997: p. 48).

People are not likely to be explicit about the inferred aspect of schemas. In normal situations, people are extremely unlikely to tell you that restaurants are places where you eat. This knowledge is so smoothly and quickly used that people cannot be consciously aware that they are using information stored in their mind as concept and schema as they go about their business. It is this ability to take most of the knowledge we need in order to operate fluently in the world which we may describe as 'going without saying', or as being 'only at the back of our mind'. However, this is what makes us act efficiently.

This background of the 'taken for granted' is essential for efficient action. It also enables us to be on the look out for the not totally predictable, which is what we most urgently need to pay attention to. A famous simple experiment shows this well. Subjects are shown the picture of a standard office where there is a large bunch of bananas on one of the desks. When subsequently they are asked to remember what was in the picture they usually miss out what can be expected to be in an office, e.g. chairs, but they never forget the bananas. The reason for this is simple; not only do our schemas enable us to know much more than is empirically evident, not only do they enable us not to clutter our consciousness with the obvious, they also enable us to focus and deal with what cannot be taken for granted, which is probably precisely what we should be dealing with. They are thus an essential device for fluent action.

Schema enable us to *assume* that a whole lot of other essential phenomena are present on the basis of minimal information. This is extremely useful in normal life as it enables us to get on with our lives, but it also can create a form of cognitive conservatism that can block necessary reconsiderations of previous understandings. This was shown by the original demonstration of the power of schemas by Frederick Bartlett (1932: ch. 5). He read to a group of Cambridge undergraduates a story from a Kwakiutl myth that had been collected by Boas and then asked them to recount it at later times and then at regular intervals. Not surprisingly, the students had great difficulty in remembering such a narrative since it seemed weird to them and it did not correspond in any way to the typical kind of stories they had been habituated to hearing. In other words, it did not correspond to their stored schemas. Since the students did not remember the myth very well, they kept on changing it in subsequent recalls until they had transformed it through time into the kind of story they were used to, that is, into a story that did correspond to their schemas. This stage having been reached, the story became stable and they were able to remember the greatly modified story quite easily. What had happened was that the schema had formed a kind of screen between what had been read to them originally and what they were able to retain. They could not hold the myth in mind as it had been told to them but once the story had been transformed, they remembered it easily. By then, it had become the kind of story they were used to and it was not the Kwakiutl text any longer.

Bartlett's experiment is extremely relevant for a topic that has become ever more important in recent social science. Anthropologists, in particular, have concentrated on the growing 'globalisation' of the world and such work can help us understand what the exposure to foreign material means. What the study of schema should suggest to social scientists is that such contact involves a much less easy flow than we might think because of the drag these large concepts operate. The Bartlett experiment means that it might be too easy to assume that people with a totally different cultural background will be greatly affected in their ideas about the world by the impact of such things as foreign television and soaps since it warns us that the effect of such inputs might not be so straightforward. Before great cultural change is brought about by exposure to a foreign media, it needs to be absorbed and taken in and this may only occur with great difficulty. The students who heard the Kwakiutl myth understood the narrative but they could not retain it and make it their own. What they ultimately retained was in fact just the type of thing they had been habituated to. If this is also true for the watchers of a foreign soap opera, we need to study – before making any assumptions, and like Bartlett did – not only the fact of exposure to exotic material, but also what people's schema enable them to retain from what they have been exposed to through time.

Where do our concepts and schemas come from?

Concepts and schemas are a constitutive part of the processes of the blob but where do they come from? Like the blob itself, they are created by a variety of fundamentally different processes, some internal and some external, all of which come together in a single continually transforming unity. To a certain extent, this is true of all animate beings except that, in the case of *Homo sapiens*, we have the added element that humans are a kind of animal that, to an extent, is also made by history and the social. The discussion of the blob in the last chapter has shown how, at any one moment, human beings are caught in two very different continuities. One is internal and involves such things as the continuity of factors such as what makes us able to locate our body in space to the fact that we can utter propositions in language; the other continuity is that which exists between individuals. The first continuity explains why anthropologists cannot do without natural science and especially cognitive science; the second continuity explains why natural scientists cannot do without social sciences. The internal continuity has been stressed in the previous chapters because this is what social scientists tend to forget but bearing it in mind also changes the way we should consider the way people make each other through social interaction.

The continuity between individuals could be called the cultural process were it not for the fact that, as we saw in chapter 4, such a terminology has led, and still rapidly leads, to the misleading opposition of nature/culture which suggests the co-occurrence of two separate, distinct and incompatible systems instead of the unity which actually exists. For this reason, I prefer the term social or historical processes rather than the term 'culture' in order to understand the dynamic mechanisms by which information is passed on from one individual to another. This transmission inevitably involves social relations since the content of what is transmitted cannot be grasped independently of the social relation which makes it possible.

How fundamentally social humans are is being recognised more and more by biologists, to the extent that several have argued that the most characteristic adaptations of our species, especially the large frontal areas of our brain, are the product of the adaptation to the complexity of human social lives (Dunbar 1997; Humphrey 2007). Furthermore, a number of evolutionary psychologists have demonstrated a very early innate propensity in human infants to act in a pro-social way (Tomasello 2009).

Even as adults, we seem programmed for co-operative shared intentional action (Knoblich and Sebanz 2008).

This social character, in so far as it is cumulative, is what enables human history, even to the extent that it dominates us as a species representing the only truly exceptional characteristic of our species. Human history is the process of social interpenetration between individuals with the added twist that the representations involved, although in a state of transformation, can be the basis of further transformations of representations occurring in long chains of communication through generations or between contemporaries. Thus, information from long ago can either be reproduced or become the basis of yet further innovations and representations.

This historical intercreation of individuals by each other occurs as people interact. It has often been represented as a system of messages passed from one individual to another. This is the metaphor that lies behind the idea of memes that was already alluded to. Such a formulation may be useful as a first step in explaining the phenomenon of culture but, as we saw, it is also misleading. First, it forgets that the individuals themselves are being created in the process. Secondly, it has been argued in the first part of this chapter that this suggests a mistakenly separable process independent of the internal continuities of the blob.

The segregation of internal processes from historical ones is misleading in a number of interrelated ways. First, it rapidly leads to a refusal to recognise just how similar humans are to other animals, especially other social animals, while, in the discussion of the core and minimal aspects of the blob in chapter 6, it was pointed out how many of the capacities involved are shared with, at the very least, other primates. Secondly, it obscures the internal continuity of key elements of what was awkwardly called the narrative self with other aspects of the blob. Thirdly, it tempts us to mistake the meta-representations of the blob for the blob itself. This is the error denounced by Galen Strawson when he stresses the need to distinguish what he calls episodics from diachronics in order not to exclude from the truly human that part of mankind which does not go in for reflecting on its autobiography. Fourthly, it forgets that transmission between individuals is a matter of continual individual transformation, absorption and creation as was stressed by Sperber and myself in our criticisms of the notion of memes (Sperber 2001; Bloch 2001). We are not dealing with an exchange of independently existing messages passed between mindless machines. Fifthly, it locates social interpenetration solely at the level of the explicit while, in fact, such exchange involves both the core and the minimal blob also. Interpenetration occurs at all levels, though to differing degrees; thus involvement in history cannot also be ruled out for these other largely inexplicit levels.

It is best to start the examination of the continuum between individuals with this last point and look at how we interpenetrate each other, and therefore, to an extent, make each other, in ways which are not specific to our species. Some of these ways are characteristic of many social species.

First of all, there is the obvious fact that all living beings are not truly distinct since genetic material is transmitted on a much longer time scale than the life span of any individual. For mammals such as us, this implies a bodily continuity as each of us is produced in the body of another and as we sexually enter, and are entered, and thus produce the longer-term continuity of the species. Perhaps this fact has not interested social and cultural anthropologists much but it should have done, at the very least, for the reason that it has furnished material for conscious meta-reflection in explicit kinship and moral discourses.

There are, however, many other ways in which we go in and out of each other's bodies. Humans, *qua* humans, feel empathy for each other and this has often been studied and demonstrated in great detail (Decety 2010). Again, it has often been noted how emotions are catching between individuals, even though we do, sometimes, attempt to resist this epidemic. Classical discussions about the power of literature and drama, going back all the way to Aristotle, are explorations of this transmission aspect of emotions. The empirical demonstrations of such emotional co-ordination are many and can be measured in terms of heart rate and skin conductivity. We are thus continually modifying each other at the most basic physiological level. Particularly interesting for anthropologists have been phenomena such as the co-ordination of heart rate between fire walkers in South American rituals with that of others closely related who are mere watchers (Konvalinka et al. 2011). There is also considerable evidence that, as we interact, our brains synchronise, and thus understanding or watching another person's actions involves much the same neurological activity as doing them oneself (Rizzolatti et al. 1996). In other words, at levels which are normally below consciousness we are continually echoing each other. The fact that we are not reflectively aware that this is going on should not make us forget that such interpenetration is part of the enabling of the historical process.

Even the apparently straightforward transmission of linguistic messages cannot be understood without placing it within psychological processes. This is implicit in the theories of Malinowski, Wittgenstein and Bourdieu discussed above. These writers rightly argue that the meaning of a word, as it would be given in a dictionary, or of a sentence out of context does not suffice for understanding use or meaning as it occurs in actual social practice. If, as they argue we should, we see utterances as a kind of action, we must consider, as is the case for all action, the presence of a multi-layered mental process which has enabled this use to occur. Furthermore, this mental process needs to be taken into account. As the pragmatists have stressed, we use words as devices that enable us to *guess* the processes in each other's mind that have led to the utterances to be made. The lexical or grammatical aspect of words and sentences has no existence other than as a mental phenomenon. It is just one tool, among others, that enables us to read the mind of each other and so decipher them. A much-used example shows this in perhaps an over simple way concerning a simple request from one person to another asking for a cup of coffee. In a case such as this we might well think that the words 'a cup of coffee' stands for a cup of coffee and that that is all there is to it. However, the person who made the request would be quite taken aback if she was presented with a cup full of coffee beans. This would be ridiculous but, if we thought the use of the words indicated nothing else than the dictionary entry for coffee, such a bizarre action would be reasonable. Of course, we know it is not reasonable because we read the speaker's mind and therefore know that what she actually intended by the use of the word. It is the full intention and motivation of the speaker, itself below the level of their consciousness, that needs to be equally unconsciously realised by the hearer for communication to take place. This is not a matter of deciphering the words as though they were hieroglyphs from a long dead civilisation. Bringing a cup of drinkable coffee is what reasonable people do in context of situation and this is what ethnographers seek to understand.

This means that when anthropologists are doing field work or when writing ethnography, what they are trying to capture is the flow of mental concepts and schema and of mind reading that occurs in social situations. Words are mere insufficient pointers and ambiguous cues for indicating the phenomena that concern them. Words have a role in helping understanding but, as Malinowski stressed, so do also many other implicit factors.

The transmission of information of concepts and schemas between and through people, which is what enables the phenomenon of history to occur, is first of all a bodily and mental process within which it occurs. Quite apart from social communication, there is yet another element in the complex process of the continual creation of human knowledge that needs to be taken into account and that is the input that comes from the external world. However, we must not forget, when considering this factor, that, as always, it is the unified multiplicity of determinations which needs to be taken into account in order to answer the question of where concepts and schemas come from.

One aspect of Malinowski's insistence on the embedding of meaning within activity is the fact that our activity on the world is part of the world. This means that concepts and schemas cannot be separate from it and its processes. These include processes which have an existence that is quite independent of the historically specific ideas we might have about them. These are processes such as, for example, the reproductive mechanisms of the plants and animals, including humans, and other processes on which we rely for our survival. This does not mean that human thought or concepts and schemas reflect the world and its dynamic but that these must mesh with it in a way that is much more direct than many anthropologists are often willing to admit.

The co-determination of concepts and schemas by the world takes place in the short term and also in the very long term. The short-term determination comes from the simple fact that concepts and schemas have to be effective in the world and therefore synchronised with it. What this means, however, is not as straightforward as it might at first seem. This is because the world we live in is not completely exterior to us; it is a world that has been, and is being, created by us and other human beings and thus it too is partly a historical phenomenon. For example, we live in houses that are made in a specific way by us and others. The specific character of these houses can only be explained if we take into account the social and cultural process that has led to the specificities of these particular places in these particular times. However, in order for the human species to survive, history has also had to take into account the requirements of physics, chemistry, social life and biology. The necessity which these different factors impose is true of all our interactions with the environment. Most importantly, this short-term meshing of our schemas and concepts with external phenomena has to occur to enable us to co-operate with other individuals whose behaviour is also, at the same time, the product of the combination of a specific history and a uniquely human psychology and physiology.

There is also a determination of concepts and schemas by the world which occurs on a much longer time scale. We have minds which have been created to be as they are by the process of natural selection.

Our minds have had to be adapted so that we have survived up to now. Our minds have therefore been made as a result of the meshing of humans in the environment, the world and its natural requirements in the long term. The basic understandings of time and causation discussed in chapter 5 are cases in point. Essentialised concepts, such as have been discussed above, also are probably, directly or indirectly, examples of the type of phenomena that natural selection has inscribed in our genome and which therefore have been made to appear to our conscious mind to be 'obvious' and not needing explanation so that they cannot be challenged. There is, however, a complication that must be taken into account when we stress the adapted character of certain aspects of our cognition. The kind of mind we have is the product of millions of years of evolution. Even if we only take into account our history as the species *Homo sapiens*, we are talking about more than 150,000 years. Thus, as has been pointed out again and again by Tooby and Cosmides (1990), during more than 99 per cent of that time our ancestors lived in small groups relying on hunting and gathering. This means that, given the very slow rate of biological evolution, it is likely that our minds, our concepts and our schemas have been, significantly, adapted for this kind of prehistoric life. Perhaps this is of no great significance for the most foundational aspects of our cognition and mind reading. However, for some other aspects of social and practical cognition it might well be, as Tooby and Cosmides argue, that our minds are out of sync with the contemporary world within which we live because natural selection has not kept up with the speed of history.

Should anthropologists despair?

This chapter has stressed the essential importance of phenomena which are either difficult or downright impossible to observe from the outside. If this is so for observation this must be also so when we consider the possibility of recording such processes. It is not entirely unknown for ethnographers to recognise the need to assume the presence of a hidden implicit level. We saw how Leach argues that we should not take explicit statements concerning virgin birth at face value and that these rest on knowledge derived from another implicit level of understanding. Similarly, in the previous chapter I showed how statements about temporality made by the Nuer or on Gawa should be considered as resting on an implicit understanding of temporality. However, it is less clear how the ethnographer can demonstrate that this implicit level is actually present in the mind of the people studied and/or that she has access to it.

As an ethnographer, the anthropologist may be tempted to despair as a result of the realisation that what is necessary for the job seems unavailable to the social science observer. This, however, is too pessimistic a view. One way out of the predicament had already been suggested by Malinowski through what he called participant observation. There have been many criticisms of participant observation, particularly of its anecdotal character, but the incredible power of its methodology for science has not been sufficiently stressed. As we saw, Malinowski presents matters in the introduction of his wonderful book *Argonauts of the Western Pacific* in a way that links the need for the awareness of the implicit which is present in practice theory with the type of research method he advocates. This is long-term interaction between the researcher and the people studied. The effect of such social interaction, as is the case with any sustained interaction between human beings, is the mutual colonisation of the related minds as people understand each other ever better. This interaction enables participants to reconstruct in their own minds the implicit that lies behind the explicit that they can observe from the behaviours and words of those with whom they are in interaction. What lies behind concepts and schemas gets known by a process of minute, very rapid and continual mind reading. This is a process of mutual colonisation of minds referred to above. The knowledge so obtained is not necessarily, nor need be, accessible to consciousness. What matters is that efficient interaction occurs between the anthropologist and the people she studies so that understanding occurs. This interpenetration is a fundamental aspect of our species (Bloch 2008). The irresistible process of reading each other's minds as we interact and participate in social life occurs because we are members of a social species whose mind has been made by natural selection for, above all, managing social relations. We are thus continually seeking to, and succeeding in, reading each other's minds and recognising and catching each other's emotions whether we want to or not. The participant observer is simply exposing her mind so that the process can take place. What Malinowski is suggesting therefore is that we use this mind reading ability as a research tool. In fact, it is probably the only one easily available if we really want to understand the motives and understandings of others in the full complexity of ordinary life at any depth. The richness of the anthropological literature shows that this can work very well.

The reason why this works so well as a research tool is not quite as simple as it seems at first. What participant observation creates is an implicit understanding by the ethnographer of the implicit in others. The problem is that what the ethnographer has learnt of the implicit of others is very difficult to present in an explicit form for the benefit of readers of monographs. This is because doing so denatures it but also because it is difficult to demonstrate to the reader of ethnography that what is claimed is indeed present. The solution is one that makes many social and cognitive scientists very uncomfortable. It consists in the claim that the way to know the implicit in those one is studying is through the ethnographer's own introspection. In other words, the ethnographer can claim that because interaction causes mutual colonisation a reflection on oneself after having been colonised is a discovery of others (Bloch 2008). Though introspection has a bad name, especially in the social and cognitive sciences, the fact that that is how much ethnography is done is often disguised. I believe, however, that there is nothing to be ashamed of, but this does not mean that we cannot also attempt to monitor this dangerous process as best we can, for example, by means of inferential tests that supplement but do not substitute for participant observation.[6] Above all, however, it is by reflecting on the processes of the character and use of implicit knowledge that we can best attempt to understand its significance and presence (Astuti 2009). This has been a central purpose of this chapter.

---

[6] The work of Astuti and myself with Carey and Solomon are examples of this (Bloch, Carey and Solomon 2000; Astuti, Carey and Solomon 2004).

EIGHT

Memory

Memory, working memory and the implicit in practice

The point of this chapter is to show how the type of arguments that have been presented up to here modify a topic which social and cultural anthropologists, as well as other social scientists, have discussed extensively. This modification is not a matter of dismissal of the work of these disciplines but rather a reformulation. Chapter 6 concluded by stressing how human beings exist within two continuities. One is internal and extends from levels of being that are normally totally inaccessible to consciousness to the fully explicit and even the meta-representational. The other continuity is that which is created by the interpenetration of individuals which allows different individuals continually to transform each other. Our knowledge, including our concepts and schemas, derive from a multiplicity of sources both internal and external and, as we saw in the previous chapter, this knowledge is more or less explicit and more or less accessible to consciousness. This chapter will consider how it is stored.

Memory in the individual has inevitably the same layered character as the blob or the knowledge examined in the earlier chapters. Information is similarly stored in similarly varied forms ranging from the implicit to the explicit and from the totally inaccessible to the fully accessible to consciousness. This information can be internal and bounded within the individual or it can be shared. When it is widely shared it becomes the phenomenon that anthropologists have traditionally called 'culture'. However, throughout this book, for reasons discussed in chapter 4, I have avoided the term. This has been because although the term helps us focus on the continuity between individuals it makes us, at the same time, forget the internal continuity. By contrast, I have stressed how both continuities must be thought together since this is how we actually are.

An introduction to memory

The topic of memory is one where we would have thought there would exist an easy link between social sciences such as anthropology, sociology and history and the cognitive sciences since both have discussed the subject many many times. The English word memory evokes a psychological phenomenon; the inscription of information in the mind or the brain which can then be retrieved at a later moment. It is not surprising therefore that psychologists and neurologists have seen the study of memory as one of their central concerns. However, social scientists too, historians, sociologists, anthropologists and even also politicians, have recently talked a great deal about memory. This is so to the extent that several writers have said, with a degree of irony, that there exists a veritable memory industry.

The question, however, is whether the different disciplines have been talking about similar things or whether they have been using the same word to refer to quite different phenomena. It would seem that this second alternative is the right one since psychologists refer to internal individual processes of the nervous system while social scientists refer to processes that in no way exist solely, or principally, in the head. Thus, social scientists will use the label memory to discuss such things as organised public commemorations or the celebration of significant events such as battles, victories or revolutions. In this sense of the word, the commemoration of the taking of the Bastille on the fourteenth of July in

France, the Passover meal of the Jews evoking the crossing of the Red Sea by the ancient Israelites, Martin Luther King day in the USA have all been called 'acts of memory'. Even buildings such as the triumphal arches of the Romans or the tombs of the pharaohs are also said to be 'about' memory. Some have even suggested that simply acting out traditional rituals, which the participants know have been done in that same way in the past by their ancestors, are forms of memory (Nora 1984). The recounting of stories about the past, especially official stories such as are found in history books or inscribed on monuments, are likewise often discussed in social science texts as part of the general topic. It also follows that, for writers such as these, the non-evocation of the past is about 'forgetting'. Thus Carsten in an article about a fishing village in Malaysia considers the lack of reference to family migration histories in general conversations as deliberate forgetting (Carsten 1995).[1] These extremely loose uses of the word 'memory' and the fact that social and cognitive scientists seem to use it for quite unrelated phenomena would seem to be good reason for not attempting to put these different types of studies together and to let the different authors continue blithely to ignore each other as they, in most cases, seem to have done.

However, in spite of the apparent dissimilarities of topics referred to under this single label of memory, the abandonment of an attempt at greater co-operation would be a lost opportunity. Perhaps some purely psychological, neurological, sociological, historical and anthropological studies can be left in peace in their own world but many writers in anthropology, sociology or history, as well as some psychologists, rightly feel that there is a connection between public manifestations, or the absence of them, and the mental phenomena that the words memory and forgetting evoke in the cognitive sciences. Exactly how this could be so is often little examined, largely because such laudable encouragements

---

[1] See Trouillot 1995: pp. 14–16 for a very interesting critique of the equation of non-evocation and forgetting.

at cross disciplinarity usually do not explore very precisely how such a difficult link could be created. The dangerous vagueness that characterises the topic is an example of the kind of psychological imprecision that characterises much of social and cultural anthropology and which this book seeks to dispel. Most cognitive scientists for their part see little point in considering non-psychological matters when talking of memory but, as will be argued below, this too is misleading.

The loose use of the word memory to refer to so many different things has been unhelpful. However, this chapter will show that it is in trying to understand the *relation* of the mental and the social that many of the topics which have been central for much work in subjects such as anthropology can be advanced. In fact, the questions that seem to lie behind most work on memory in subjects such as history and anthropology are: what relationship, if any, exists between what is stored in our head and externally observable public events?

This chapter will be primarily concerned with memory as an internal psychological phenomenon. Nonetheless, these subjects, although usually discussed by psychologists, also have great anthropological significance and when this is taken into account the whole topic is enriched. The second half of this chapter, by contrast, will focus on issues which have been traditionally central in the social sciences and show how these also are moved forward by an informed cognitive perspective.

Working memory, procedural memory and habitus

If we are to bring social scientific and cognitive studies in relation with each other this necessitates being clear about the meaning of the words we shall have to use. The terms concerned with memory will be used here in the way they are defined by psychologists since they have been much more careful in distinguishing these than the social scientists. Thus, for the sake of clarity I here only use the word *memory* and verbs such as *remembering* for the inscription of information about the past in the nervous system of individuals. Acts involving consciously recognising information from the past will be called *recollecting*. When remembering involves expressing the content of this knowledge to others in language the word *recalling* will be used. Finally, when talking of acts or speech about events in the past which are not clearly linked with individual memory of these events I shall use the word *evoking*.

The psychological study of memory is a huge subject that can only be touched on in a book such as this. As we saw in the previous chapter, we need memory for such basic cognitive processes as using concepts. The concept indicated by the word cat makes us able to recognise that the animal in front of us can be said to be a cat. To do this, we must consequently have stored in memory information and theories about that sort of animal in the form of a concept. We need memory of the beginning of a sentence in order to complete it successfully. We need memory for time travel as discussed in chapter 5. We need memory to organise tasks in a purposeful manner. We need to remember information that we have learnt throughout life, what was called in chapter 6 the narrative level, in order to be an efficient adult member of society. We need to hold mental maps in our head in order to find our way around and we need to remember such things as a dentist's appointment that will take place at a future time. We need to remember that water consists of H2O in order to pass exams, and so on. These memories are clearly of different types. They may be about the distant past or not experienced as being about the past at all. They may be stored throughout life or only for a short while. They may be explicit in that we can express them in language and be aware that we hold them, or implicit and difficult, or even downright impossible to drag to the surface of consciousness whether this recall takes a linguistic or other form of public manifestation.

Because of this enormous multiplicity of types of memory, psychologists have had to draw distinctions between memory systems and it has very often turned out that the types of memories they so distinguished, at first simply on the basis of introspection and some experimental data, have turned out to correspond to different patterns of activation of different parts of the brain and can therefore be said to be neurologically fairly distinct.

One fundamental distinction that has been made in this way is between shorter-term memory systems involved in such actions as remembering from beginning to end what one is up to when performing a practical task – for example, combing one's hair – from longer-term memory involved in remembering, for example, what one did on one's twenty-first birthday or when one's favourite football team last won a match.

Short-term memory is usually assumed to be of little interest to social scientists largely because the experiments that were used to study it have little to do with real situations and involve tasks totally divorced from ordinary life such as remembering nonsense syllables in laboratory settings. Such studies may indeed have little interest as such for anthropologists and historians, but short-term working or procedural memory is closely linked to our ability to perform familiar tasks, a capacity that should be of interest to social scientists. This becomes clear when the notion of short-term memory is further refined by the label 'working memory' (Baddeley 1986) because the performance of work and practice are regularly acknowledged as a central aspect of what social scientists study.

In any case, even if different types of memory are distinguished they connect seamlessly with each other. Thus, the performance of everyday tasks requires the integration of longer-term knowledge with the intentionality of the moment. That this occurs has, for a long time now, been a central topic of interest in a subject such as anthropology as scholars have focussed on the everyday practices and performance of familiar tasks (de Certeau 1980; Piette 2009). In the previous chapter, I discussed the 'practice' theories of Bourdieu and Malinowski. It is clear that the kind of position they envisaged involved uses of memory, if only through concepts and schemas.

What is striking, however, is how few actual empirical studies of 'embodiment', 'practice' or 'habitus' are reported in the social science literature whether by Bourdieu or anybody else. This is partly due to the difficulty of observing the long-term learning of tasks which then makes them become quasi-automatic but also because, as we saw, the terms are vague.

In spite of the mass of references to practice in modern social science and in spite of the grand declarations that there is something called 'practice theory', the reality is that what such a theory proposes about the nature of knowledge, how it is learnt and how it is stored, never goes beyond the vaguely metaphorical implied by phrases such as that it is 'embodied', as though this could occur elsewhere than in the nervous system. The insistence by writers, often by writers influenced by the phenomenological tradition in philosophy of the need to take all aspects into account has often simply led to the abandonment of any analysis because the task becomes overwhelming.

The basis of the problem is that the normal methods of the social sciences do not enable us to go beyond the merely superficial in the attempt to understand what is being pointed towards by words such as habitus and embodiment. What is at issue is knowledge in practice which takes a form that resists the methods and style of explanation which are typical of subjects such as anthropology and traditional philosophy. The arguments of practice theories often simply turn out to be ways of saying that what is being talked about is difficult to talk about.

A partial exception to this has been the work by a number of anthropologists on apprenticeship. These anthropologists (Goody 1978; Lave and Wenger 1991) were struck by the lack of explicit teaching in this way of transferring knowledge and the discouragement of the learner asking questions of the master. This method of transfer of practical knowledge is quite unlike the method used in school contexts. It is expected that, somehow, through hanging around expert craftsmen such as weavers, learning occurs through a process that Lave and Wenger call legitimate peripheral participation. Knowledge seems to *seep* into the apprentice, but it takes a very long time to do so.

One of the reasons why the work on apprenticeship is important is that it is clear that this type of peripheral learning is not limited to apprenticeship but is probably typical of the way much practical and everyday knowledge is passed on. However, when we want to begin to go beyond the surface phenomena and try to understand what is involved in the way knowledge taken in from external stimuli is then transformed so that it can be used with fluency, we have to turn to quite different theories from those of the practice anthropologists.

This is of course not an accident. Anthropological field work, especially participant observation, is excellent at making one aware of the presence of the implicit in the social and at making one realise how meaning cannot be separated from social interaction. Like Malinowski, the ethnographer intuits how language carries meaning only in the 'context of situation' and going with this is the feeling that knowledge is transferred implicitly through peripheral participation. Malinowski, and to a certain extent other anthropologists, are expert at passing on these intuitions to the readers of their ethnographies, but, as was argued in the previous chapter, by obtaining help from subjects such as cognitive psychology and neurology we can understand practice in greater depth.

The knowledge that we use in ordinary practical tasks is difficult to talk about for a relatively simple reason although this is rarely faced frontally in the social sciences. The reason is that we have to access our knowledge extraordinarily fast and fluently. This fact rules out the possibility of the actor being conscious of the process by which she acts or of the knowledge on which her actions are based. The actor does not necessarily know that she knows nor what she knows, nor how she has acquired her knowledge. This is not a problem for the actor herself but it is a problem for the social scientist who is always tempted to base her ethnographic account on what the people she studies can explain. This problem lies at the root of Malinowski's criticism of the interview as the basic method of ethnography. His criticisms are expanded by Bourdieu and Wittgenstein as we saw in the previous chapter. However, the problem with these writers' strictures is that, although they understand well the difficulty, they propose very little in ways by which we can go deeper in cornering what it is that makes practical knowledge implicit in action and therefore ethnographically unmanageable. If they, very justifiably, attempt, as most ethnographers do, to produce accounts that make us intuit the point of view of the actor, they are obstructed in justifying their apparently loose procedures by the fact that the actor cannot say why he does what he does and is unable to explain why this is so. The causes of the obstruction are that knowledge and the production of actions in the brain are organised totally differently to the way narrative accounts are organised. This was implicit in the criticisms made by Galen Strawson of the over-narrative accounts of the self found in such writers as Dennett and Ricoeur and which I took on board in chapter 6. It is implicit in Malinowski's demand that the anthropologist participates in order to understand and does not base himself merely on interviews. However, we need to move from the negative to more positive suggestions. To understand this non-narrative type of organisation, we need to search beyond the usual methods and points of view of the social sciences and seek help from the cognitive sciences.

This is why in different publications Strauss and Quinn and I have stressed the relevance for anthropology of psychological and neurological theories and research about the working of the brain when we want to deal with the implicit. This work can help us account for the fluency of practice and the difficulty of rendering it in linguistic form. In particular, we have discussed an approach to the working of the brain called connectionism (Bloch 1991; Strauss and Quinn 1997).

Connectionism

Connectionism is a controversial neurological theory, several aspects of which are particularly relevant for social science. The first concerns the way knowledge stored in the brain is used. Particularly revealing is the fact that considerable psychological and neurological experimental work shows that humans, and not only humans, are able to take in information from a number of perceptual sources *in parallel* and to integrate these sources in the very processes of perception and cognition, as, for example, when we combine auditory and visual signals in order to understand linguistic communications. Even if we limit ourselves to the examination of a single sense, sight for example, we find that we are able to take in and process information from many distinct sources as we simultaneously make sense of the situation.

The connectionist explanation of why this feat of taking in information simultaneously from different types of perception is possible is the second reason why social scientists should pay attention to the theory. The connectionists suggest that instead of knowledge being stored in linear sentential fashion it becomes reorganised in webs of networks connected in a multitude of ways. These resemble, because of their complexity and complex connectivity, the appearance of interconnected neurons in the nervous system. Whatever the significance of this resemblance, it suggests the possibility that such connected networks could receive and analyse the multiple simultaneous information which comes from perception and match it to equally complex and connected cognitive processes. This parallel processing would enable the cognitive fluency and extraordinary cognitive speed which characterises the way we live our lives and which, as we saw in the last chapter, presents a challenge to natural language-like and single-level accounts of cognition suggested in typical ethnography. For example, an expert farmer is able, at a glance, to know the agricultural potential of a piece of land he has just come across for the first time. To do this feat, apparently effortlessly, he must simultaneously take in a great variety of information in parallel and mesh this with concepts and schemas stored in memory. For such a feat to be possible, not only is perception necessarily organised in a form like that of the connectionist model, it is likely that conceptual and schematic knowledge is also stored in the mind in connectionist form. This means that the discussion of the various types of concepts and schemas considered in the previous chapter may have to be reformulated so as to take into account such neurological organisation since this would explain how it is that we can cope at the required speed and degree of fluency which characterises human action.

Not only could connectionism explain why it is possible that we can use our knowledge as fluently as we do, it would also explain why so much of our knowledge is accessed without our being conscious of this occurring and, therefore, why it remains implicit. The reason is quite simply that its complexity and multi-layered character is just too enormous for us to be consciously aware of its extraordinary capacity. Conscious reasoning processes would be much too slow and clumsy. By contrast the connectionist model suggests an explanation of the kind of thing which, as social scientists, we seek to understand. That is the way we act competently in the practical process of life in society. As we do this, we seem to marshal memorised information with such facility that we are unaware that we are doing so, whether this is learnt or originates from shared human understandings. Neuronal organisation of this sort would explain why information, which could be called 'cultural' since it is the product of long-term historical chains transmission, transformation and exchange, feels as though it sprang naturally and fluently from our minds as we are involved in action. Connectionism, or something like it, would thus be a neurological explanation of the phenomena that Bourdieu and Malinowski describe by such terms as practice or habitus.

And there is another aspect of connectionist theory that makes it thought-provoking for anthropologists. This concerns the relationship of knowledge acquisition to knowledge in practice, a topic to which we shall return later in this chapter. Since we are able to do the kind of feat that the evoked expert farmer can do, the question is how was it possible for such complex and largely unconscious knowledge to have been acquired since the necessary information about soils and hydrology cannot have been transferred explicitly to him by another since this other person also most probably held this knowledge in mind implicitly. Probably some of the transfer occurred through 'peripheral participation'. Saying this, however, does not make clear how the transfer actually occurred at the psychological or the neurological level; it merely tells us that it has occurred. Probably some of the transfer occurred through imitation, but yet again saying this is insufficient. Minds do not reflect each other like mirrors and so the mechanism is not explained by such a word either. Finally, there may have been some explicit transmission but this raises the question of how implicit knowledge can be transferred explicitly via a medium such as language. None of these mechanisms leads to the storage complexity and multi-connected character of knowledge that is necessary for fluent action. To understand how such knowledge is fully passed from one individual to another, we need to see that it must undergo a double transformation. The implicit connectionist network in the mind of the sender of information will have to be transformed into a simpler, much more language-like type of communication, if not into language itself, if the sender intends to communicate. And, even if the sender has no such intention, the receiver will have to transform back the information from what can be detected from the environment, which will include the messages intentionally sent by the sender, into the connected systems necessary for human action. We are helped in understanding these processes of transformation from the more explicit into the more implicit and back again by a number of cognitive studies concerning the learning of skills like those of an expert farmer. Such skills become so embedded in ourselves that we are unaware that we are using them. Many of these are influenced by connectionism. Studies on chess experts and more mundanely car drivers show what might be involved (Johnson-Laird 1983). In both cases, the process of learning is not a gradual process. Instead, it is, at first, one of slow progress followed by sudden leaps forward. This initial irregularity of absorption is probably due to the fact that the information needs to be assimilated first in its more explicit form and then reorganised in a different way for a system of storage which enables the use of stored knowledge implicitly. The connectionist model is a powerful suggestion of how this might happen; in any case some sort of transformation is necessary before knowledge can be used with the fluency characteristic of our ordinary life (Bloch 1991).

A perspective such as this highlights, once again, what is wrong with the Boasian or Dawkins's model of culture. In such a view, the knowledge we use is envisaged as a fixed, internally coherent, one-level and classificatory system. Such a system is then implicitly or explicitly envisaged as transmissible through simple reproduction and imitation. By contrast, the connectionist model, as well as what is much less clearly implied in the work of Bourdieu and Malinowski, suggests that transmission is a highly active process involving several types of transformation. This might involve the transformation of the implicit into the explicit and back again, it might involve the reformulation of the implicit into a transferable form and it might involve the storage of the explicit in a temporarily unassimilated state while waiting for such assimilation. All these processes of psychological transformation are necessary and continually occurring if knowledge from others is ultimately to be memorised and then made available at the speed which we require as we go about our lives. This creation and recreation explains how what has been called 'culture' can never be a one-level self-contained system of the mind as the word suggests. Rather, the knowledge memorised in our mind is as much a continually active transformative process occurring between different levels of the blob as the transformative process of interaction of people among themselves and with the world. Furthermore, the process going on internally in the mind and that going on externally in the world in which it occurs themselves interact but remain very independent. These linked interactions involve the continual reorganisation of external information through smooth incorporation into working memory as the memorised information is used. It is the kind of thing that Malinowski, Wittgenstein and Bourdieu were feeling for but which they did not fully approach as they lacked, or refused, the help of the advances which cognitive science provides and will continue to provide.

Perhaps the simplest but important lesson that social scientists can learn from other cognitive sciences concerning such topics is that information is stored in a form quite different from the way it is originally received (Squire 1992). The implications of this are immense since the complex processes of transformation this necessitates means that the knowledge we use and which enables us to produce action and speed simply cannot be easily accessible to explicit consciousness. This means, *inter alia*, that, for example, an anthropologist has to take into account the fact that all statements about beliefs, understandings, etc., that she may hear from informants have, necessarily, had to have been totally transformed by a very complex psychological process within the mind of the informants from the way they are inscribed in their memory so as to take a form that can be made explicit and communicable. Such statements are therefore very remote from the inner states that produce action and to which they might, at first, seem to give access to. Because of this, such statements have always to be understood as second-order interpretations, and anthropologists must treat them as such. We saw the problem of not realising this in the discussion in chapter 5, with ethnographies of time. The criticisms voiced in that chapter show how theoretically profound was Malinowski's insistence on participant observation since it is only from the observation and participation in practice that the implicit knowledge which informs action and that we use for everyday tasks can be glimpsed, but then within ourselves. Models such as connectionism can help us understand why this massive obstacle to ethnography exists.

The realisation that there is such a distance between the way information is stored and what is easily expressible shows how misleading the views of a writer such as Derrida are when he famously stated that: 'Il n'y a pas de hors texte' (there is nothing but the text). What he meant, by implication, is that we should content ourselves with the surface of what is said and done and forget about the mind that has produced it (Derrida 1967: p. 233).[2] By contrast, throughout this book it is argued that the text, if by that is meant by the explicit, is but a distant manifestation of what the social scientist wants to know and that, even that, cannot be fully grasped unless it is seen as an aspect of people's active and cognitive processes. The job of the anthropologist is to discover through various field techniques, some of which may well be borrowed from other cognitive sciences, what this hidden knowledge might be.

Longer-term memory, episodic memory and autobiographical memory

Psychologists usually distinguish between short-term memory and long-term memory. They further divide long-term memory into two kinds. One relates to what has happened to the individual concerning such events as what it was like when one first saw the Eiffel tower. They call this type of memory episodic or autobiographical memory. The other they call semantic memory. This relates to the memory that the Eiffel tower is 324 metres high, a fact one has learnt in school.

These various long-term memories are partly constitutive of the blob, especially at the minimal and narrative levels of the blob. Referring these memories to the blob, however, also makes clear that, as with all its levels, distinguishing types of memory does not rule out partial merging. The example of the Eiffel tower shows this as it is quite probable that memory of the first time one saw it may be inseparable from what was learnt

---

[2] This phrase has been interpreted in many bizarre ways that I ignore here.

in school. This lack of absolute separation between externally obtained information and more internal processes demonstrates once again the coexistence of the two continuities discussed in chapter 6. We shall return to this topic later in the chapter.

Similarly, the discussion in the previous section, which could be considered as only concerning short-term memory, cannot be completely separated from discussion of the longer-term memories involved in the blob. This link, as we shall see, has led to terminological problems with the terms 'episodic' and 'autobiographical' memory.

In turning to this subject, we are leaving behind short-term memory considered earlier in this chapter and moving to a consideration of long-term memory and more particularly autobiographical memory. There is, however, a bridge between short-term memory and autobiographical memory and this has usually been discussed with the term episodic memory used in a new sense.

Working and procedural memory, discussed in the previous sections of this chapter, are some of the mechanisms that enable us to act in terms of information that we are not conscious of using and which we would normally never express explicitly. Working memory requires short-term operational memory but we also need longer-term, though not very long-term memories, to achieve our goals. This type of memory which links with the totality of single tasks or episodes has been called episodic memory (Tulving 1972). This, like working memory, seems fairly clearly localisable in the occipital region of the brain (Conway 2001).

At first, the terms episodic memory and autobiographical memory were used synonymously, but more recently some scholars, such as Martin Conway, have distinguished the two. For such authors, episodic memory organises actions within a fairly clearly defined 'episode' that lasts a few hours at most and in many cases much less. These chunks of limited-term memories are not necessarily stored in longer-term memory and permanently retained. Such episodic memory is not normally the subject of recall. If we imagine the farmer, evoked in the last chapter, going to his field in the morning, taking in information of the state of things, deciding on the tasks needing to be done during the day, organising his plan of action and getting on with the job, the continuity that enables him to follow the plan comes from the fact that he has constructed a memory of the episode that is both of what he has done and what he plans to do. Such memory is concerned with the task; therefore it does not necessarily or normally need to be retained in the long run. In such cases, it would remain inexplicit. This is, in Conway's terminology, an episodic memory.

Thus, such episodic memory goes hand in hand with working memory and its processes are, as noted in the previous section of this chapter, what the word 'habitus' or 'practice' in the writing of social scientists seems to point to. However, episodic memory is important for another reason, equally relevant to the anthropologist and historian. This is because it is linked with autobiographical memory.

Autobiographical memory

The specificity of autobiographical memory must also be treated as problematic because the most contentious issues have already been touched on in the discussion of the blob in chapter 6. The topic of autobiographical memory is one that has been central for social sciences such as anthropology, sociology or history, but within these disciplines it is usually discussed in ways that make its psychological status uncertain. One obstacle is that, while cognitive scientists are concerned with remembering as it is defined above, social scientists often mix this with a discussion of recalling. We already came across this problem in the discussion of what, in chapter 6, was called the narrative self. This is because very often the notion of the narrative self and autobiographical memory merge and are seen as two sides of the same coin, although, as we shall see, other levels of the blob are also involved. This is largely unproblematic if we link autobiographical memory to the narrative self in the sense of the top, non-meta-representational level of the blob, something which all humans possess whether they are, in Strawson's terms, 'episodics' or 'diachronics'. The association of the narrative level of the blob with autobiographical memory would, however, become problematic if by narrative self we meant the meta-representations that only diachronics go in for. This is because, as with the term narrative, it is important to distinguish two senses of the uses of the term autobiographical memory. In the first sense, which I retain, autobiographical memory is not about recall. Everyone has autobiographical memory whether one goes in for memory talk or not. However, in the second misleading sense, autobiographical memory is that which Strawson's diachronics go in for which is quite a different matter since this is only manifested in the act of recalling and perhaps also in the act of recollecting. This chapter will return to such recallings and there it will be called meta-autobiographical memory. The discussion of autobiographical memory below only concerns the non-meta-representational phenomenon and the top level of the blob itself.

It is perhaps best to approach autobiographic memory through a reflection on the most general question of all. What is the evolutionary significance of an awareness of cognitive continuity for the individual? The need for awareness that one is the same phenomenon through time seems to be a necessary prerequisite for the storage of knowledge about the world, knowledge that, in turn, can inform future action. There is thus a connection between autobiographical memory and the other main type of long-term memory that psychologists distinguish: semantic memory learnt from others, for example, that the chemical composition of water is H_2O. Obviously, all one's semantic knowledge, apart from innate knowledge, ultimately derives from episodes in one's autobiography; that is, it must have been learnt at some time during one's life, and is therefore, in some way, related to autobiography. Autobiographical memory is necessary for any and all social relations. These obviously require awareness that one is the same person through time and also that one is aware that others are the same persons through time. So, a kind of implicit autobiography needs to be built up and is present at the level of the minimal blob. This gradual building up of such an autobiography probably occurs in other animals than *Homo sapiens* in order to anchor what they learn in time (Skowronski and Sedikides 2007). Autobiographical memory seems particularly necessary for social animals since they need some sort of awareness of their own continuity and the continuity of others in order to interact with them with a degree of predictability. Such autobiographical memory need not be, nor is usually, available to consciousness. It is built up through putting together only certain episodic memories that are retained. Because of the connection between episodic memory and autobiographical memory, many psychologists, such as Tulving (Tulving 1985), have used the terms autobiographical memory and episodic memory interchangeably. However, equating the two obscures the fact that autobiographical memory is built up of only certain selected relevant episodic memories. Those episodic memories that are not inscribed in autobiographical memory are simply not retained for the long term (Conway 2005). This selection process of episodic memories for the building up of autobiographical memory is complex and could be of great significance for social scientists. It should be an ideal ground for co-operation between social scientists and psychologists. However, before this can occur it is necessary to disentangle some over-easy assumptions, that have become accepted in disciplines such as anthropology and sociology, which suggest that memory, and therefore the selection process of episodic memories, is simply a by-product of social circumstances.

The interrelation of autobiographical memory with specific social contexts will be examined in the latter part of this chapter but it is important to remember that other factors, such as emotional intensity of the original experience or the age at which the events occurred, also explain the selection of episodic memories retained for autobiographical memory (Williams and Conway 2009).

Halbwachs and collective memory

The beginning of this chapter emphasised how the word memory has been used for all sorts of things and the consequent need to distinguish between remembering, recollecting, recalling and evoking. This, however, does not mean that there are no significant connections between remembering, recalling and even evoking. This section focusses on these issues and more particularly as they relate to the question of autobiography.

The connection between what these different terms indicate is indirect and can only be studied if the distinctions are clear; however, much writing in the social sciences, especially in anthropology, seems to have deliberately cultivated the muddles which collapsing these terms creates. The very widespread use of the notion of 'collective memory' in these disciplines is a case in point.

The term 'collective memory' is often traced back to a book by Maurice Halbwachs entitled in English *On Collective Memory* (Halbwachs 1925). Halbwachs was a disciple of Durkheim and a key point of Durkheim's sociology was that persons were the product of the organisation of the society in which they live, not the other way round as is commonly assumed. For Durkheim, the person could be seen both in terms of her place in the social system and in terms of subjective experience, but for him the two were assumed to reflect each other. Halbwachs argued that this subjective experience depended on autobiographical memory, and so by demonstrating that autobiographical memory was a *social* product Halbwachs was proving the thesis of his teacher. The subjective individual, or person, or self, were, by means of this argument, shown to be the product of society. Since so many subsequent social scientists subscribe to a Durkheimian view of the blob or similar ones found in the texts of certain Marxists writers and also in those of the more recent Foucauldian ones, the Halbwachsian view of autobiographical memory is particularly attractive to many. This is also the case for less theoretical anthropological writers that may not refer to autobiographical memory specifically but who also assume, without much examination, that memory is the same kind of phenomenon as self-justifying evocations of the more distant past spoken by those who may, or may not, have had first-hand experience of the events concerned, since these may well have occurred long before their birth. The claim made by these theoreticians is that 'memory' is created by the social or cultural context within which it is expressed. For example, Malinowski sees stories about the past merely as 'charters' for present social organisation (Malinowski 1926). He thereby implies that, as the social situation changes, stories would be modified accordingly. Even more radically, Bohannan tells us that among the Tiv, a west African people, genealogies are smoothly changed to take into account shifts in power and demographic weight (Bohannan 1952). Similarly, Leach claims that Kachin accounts of history, whether autobiographical or referring to a time further back, are really only thinly disguised 'claims to land' (Leach 1954). In anthropology, such arguments are legion. They can be called functionalist in that they imply that the function of a statement, e.g. demonstrating a right to a piece of land is what creates the content of the discourse.

When we look at Halbwachs's position more closely, the problems with such arguments, especially as they relate to the topic of memory, become clear since he is much more explicit and much more aware of the difficulties entailed than many others.

Halbwachs uncontroversially maintained that the evocation of the past in the discourse of any one person when speaking to others is a social act and is therefore not merely governed by what one has stored in the brain about the past, but also by the micro political intentions and relative power of the participants as well as by their concepts of what is 'appropriate' for the particular context in which these discourses occur. That these social factors are significant for the act of recall is clear but the question that remains is how significant they are and what they mean for memory. This problem is faced frontally by Halbwachs; he claimed that all recollections whether public or even unspoken are similarly moulded by the social. Thus, according to him, the individual, even when alone, is as though addressing an imaginary audience of people who are socially relevant for her. For Halbwachs, therefore, it does not matter whether we are thinking by ourselves or addressing others; the social contextual constraints on what is evoked always apply and so the social moulds the content of 'memory'. Finally, Halbwachs assumes that because we are still in a social context, even when thinking in private, we can only *remember* what the social context allows us to recall.

It is necessary to examine this argument step by step precisely because, as noted above, Halbwachs-like arguments are so common in the social sciences.

The social moulding of memory

First of all, we find implicit in this argument the basic idea that auto-biographical memory is stored in the mind in a language-like form and that, therefore, the recalling of this memory can simply be a matter of its 'coming out' into the light of day when it is spoken. As argued through-out the book, this unexamined implicit idea is extremely common in the social sciences, though as discussed in chapter 6 this is quite wrong. It is also what leads to the mistake that Galen Strawson denounced. The assumption that potentially explicit narratives about the self are mere public exposition of autobiographical memory often leads those anthro-pologists who do not find these types of narratives during their field research to assume that they are dealing with people with no interiority and no autobiography.

Thus, anthropologists, ignoring the problems concerning the nature of the storage of knowledge in the brain, are able to assume that they can 'read' the autobiographical memory of those they study in their narratives about the past. They do this because they merge memory and recall while these are quite different types of things. Memorised knowledge is not only not language-like, but it cannot be for two reasons. First, it is made up of retained episodic memories which are themselves linked to action sequences of which the linguistic acts are only a part of what Malinowski or Bourdieu would call 'embodied' knowledge. Secondly, memorised knowledge cannot be language-like as it is used in practice with the fluency which characterises ordinary life.

Thus, whatever relation exists between autobiographical memory and social and other contexts is complex and, with the present state of knowledge, we can only be tentative. Obviously, what happens to the individual and what may, therefore, be potentially stored in memory depends on the kind of life one leads. But, once episodes from that life have been stored they become much less malleable than is often believed by social scientists (Boyer 2009). There is most probably a social factor involved in the choice of which episodic memories are selected for storage, although, once the selection has occurred, there seems little possibility of modification. This means that the social factors which do affect the content of autobiographical memory relate to the time when the memories are stored and not to the time when, and if, they are recalled. The easy reactive adaptation of memory to the social conditions *at the time of recall*, which is implied in Halbwachs's theory and in functionalist explanations, simply does not occur.

There is, however, a longer-term possible effect of outside influences on autobiographical memory. It has often been noted, both by social scientists and psychologists, that what individuals experience as the product of a purely private autobiographical experience may well be strongly influenced by sources of information coming from other people with whom they have been in direct or indirect contact. Thus, William Christian (Christian 1998), in an article on pilgrims in ecstasy at the Fatima shrine in Spain, notes how bodily postures of which the worshipers seem hardly conscious, and which seem to these simply a manifestation of a deep mystical experience, are, in fact, strongly influenced by changing fashions in religious images, whether these be paintings or photographs. In this way, what individuals experience as coming from deep in them turns out to be, in part, the product of external representations.

There are many examples of cases where individuals have been told of something that happened to them in early childhood and that they then come to believe they remember 'first hand'. This creates the possibility that individuals may honestly 'remember' episodes that never happened to them. Piaget has given a famous example of this (Piaget 1962). He recounts how he clearly believed he remembered how, as an infant in his push chair guided by his nurse, he and her were attacked by ruffians attempting to kidnap him. The nurse, however, was able to fight off the kidnappers and so the infant Piaget was safe. This is the story that the nurse told his parents and for which she was rewarded with a watch. Such a dramatic event was often recalled within in the family circle. However, much later, the nurse filled with remorse, confessed that she had made up the story and felt she had to return the watch. Yet Piaget had been convinced, as a result of the fact that this story had been told so often, that he really could remember exactly what had happened to him and that he could 'see' the events most vividly in his mind's eye. Piaget uses this episode to highlight the permeability of our conscious memory to what is said around us and social psychology is full of similar cases.

There is no doubt that such genuine feelings of false autobiographic sentiment caused by narrative or visual exposure do occur and they have been extensively discussed, but there is yet a further reason for social scientists to be interested by this phenomenon. This is because such alterations seem to be affected in certain predictable ways by cultural schemas. As discussed in chapter 7 cultural schemas and their effect on memory were extensively discussed by Bartlett (Bartlett 1932). Cultural schema are default, familiar schema which have become accepted, largely unconsciously, among groups of people as the normal way 'things are'. These schemas, therefore, go unexpressed but they facilitate communication by allowing most things to be 'taken for granted'. Bartlett showed how these schemas have an effect on memory in that episodes that correspond to them are more easily retainable, and that, as a result, episodes are often modified to correspond to the schemas before they become fixed in memory. In this way, and in so far as schemas are culturally specific, the particular culture and group or groups in which the individual is inserted seem to create memories. If the possibility of modification is genuine, then autobiographical memory can be said, to a certain degree, not to be individual in that some aspects are affected by macro historical processes that have created the context in which individuals find themselves.

This may be so but a note of caution is necessary. The demonstration of the effect of external influences on autobiographical memory have not actually been demonstrated at the level of memory but simply at the level of recall or meta-autobiographical memory since this is normally all that is observable. This qualification is not a minor point. For example, we do not know if, after Piaget had found out that the kidnapping episode was not true, he was not then able to revisit his memory in such a way that was more in accord with what actually happened. Thus, a number of therapeutic techniques claim that they can retrieve lost memories (Hacking 1996). These claims are much disputed. If these procedures really do what they claim, it might be that false memories are simply memories that have been moulded by what the patient assumed was appropriate for the original context of recall and that subsequent recalls are memories of previous recalls while the actual original memories as stored in the brain have not been so easily modified.

The social moulding of recall

Thus, quite different considerations are relevant for the study of acts of recall that have been seen as relevant to memory. In fact, most of the time social scientists are talking about recall, but by mixing up remembering and recall they often slip sideways from recall in making unlikely claims about the extreme malleability of memory itself.

The factors affecting recall are varied. It can be assumed that recall has *some* relation to memory but of course that can only be true of those aspects of memory which are accessible to consciousness and are thus available for recollection. In this respect, it is important to remember, as noted above, that for recollection to occur at all, a great deal of translation and transformation from memory is necessary and that even further and more radical transformations of a different kind are then necessary for recollection to take on a linguistic form in recall.

Apart from its problematic relation to memory, it is clear that the social situation at the time of the linguistic act of recall affects its content. This may be so for reasons of which the speaker is conscious. There are things we are conscious of recollecting, especially about autobiography, that we are unwilling to recall in certain contexts. This may be because we want to keep these recollections hidden or because we feel they are inappropriate to the social circumstances in which the recall occurs. For example, the loose and fanciful psychoanalytic explanations for the often observed fact that survivors of horrible situations such as concentration camps or massacres do not talk about these, especially to their families, may simply be due to the fact that there exists no appropriate social context for such recall. Since contexts vary, we may refuse to recall one anecdote in one context that we may have no problem recalling in another. If for no other reason, this banal fact serves, once again, to remind us how different recalling and remembering actually are.

More interesting, however, are less conscious manipulations of recall. As for any speech act, we are continually monitoring, largely unconsciously, the other people with whom we are involved by observing their facial and bodily expressions and a myriad of other clues. We are imagining their minds imagining our minds as occurs in any social situation and continually adapting what we seek to transmit in relation to this mind-reading activity. There is no doubt that these factors are a contributing factor in determining what is said, and, in this particular case, what is recalled. However, the realisation of this fact leaves open the question whether any of this continual and fluid social adaptation of recall has any real effect on memory. Halbwachs's claim is that it does. His thesis is that the constraints put on accounts of the past by the social context of recall directly and smoothly transform memory. This is extremely unlikely given the fundamental difference in nature between remembering and recalling and the resistance of memory to easy change noted above. But, because Halbwachs and anthropologists, sociologists and historians do not distinguish between recall and remembering and because of their lack of reflection on what would be involved psychologically if radical modifications were common, this improbable idea so often slips by unexamined.

One could be tempted to dismiss such a proposition as nothing more than a product of the confusion between remembering and recalling. This probably would be a justified initial criticism in a discussion of Halbwachs's work, except that there is also some rather weak evidence that the act of recalling does have some, perhaps minor, effects on remembering. The problem, however, is that demonstrating this is very difficult since testing can only easily be done on recall. An important possibility for anthropology is that repeated recalls relate to each other rather than to the original recollection or memories. It thus becomes difficult to know whether subsequent recalls are not, in fact, simply recalls of previous recalls rather than related to the original events inscribed in memory. Such repeated recalls would therefore be above all a matter of creating a kind of 'accepted' or 'received' individual discourse about certain events, precisely the sort of thing that anthropologists are likely to be interested in, although the existence of such increasingly stereotypic discourses, contrarily to what is often believed, cannot be assumed to have a direct relation to memory. However, the possibility that it may becomes all the more interesting when we turn to the question of whether there really could be 'collective memory'.

Collective memory

Literally, the idea that a group of people can have memories is nonsense. The writers who have argued for collective memory imply that there can be some sort of shared autobiographical memory; however, if, in the simple manner of the author of this book we remember what neurological mechanisms enable autobiographical memory, it is clear that memory can only exist in one individual nervous system.

What has made the idea of collective memory semi-plausible is the power of metaphors which both social scientists and the people they study share when, for example, people talk of a nation, or a descent group, as being 'one'. Such metaphors indicate representations that can occasionally provoke subjective states. It is possible for the speakers and hearers of such rhetoric to experience these discourses sometimes as metaphoric and sometimes, usually temporarily, as literal. This is a most important and difficult subject of study. It is therefore right that the study of such statements should be of great, even central, concern for social scientists. We need to analyse the psychological phenomenon that the rhetoric of oneness implies and this may be very difficult. In any case, we should not think that because a group of people talks of being one that they actually experience being one, and we, as anthropologists, should certainly not take this ridiculous idea on board. When these discourses invade the analytical level and are talked of by scholars as if they literally referred to phenomena that exist in the world, in this case to psychological phenomena, they become unhelpful because such an approach hinders the study of the very states the participants evoke and blocks an examination of how these states might be possible.

At its most simple, what is being referred to is the synchronisation of recall within a group of people. We have already noted how, at the individual level, subsequent recalls can become synchronised with each other and become simply repetitions of narratives which are likely to become ever more stereotypic as a result of their increasing fixity. The same process occurs when such narratives are repeated by different speakers, either one after another, as in old-fashioned history lessons, or in unison, as sometimes occurs in a ritual. As such, this type of synchronisation tells us nothing about the modifications of individual memory brought about by the creation of such standard accounts or of the synchronisation of the memory of the group, though it is often assumed, in an overly easy way in the social science literature, that it does. Thus, in an earlier article I described how the existence of such a stereotypic narrative about what had happened in a standardised account had not obstructed the production of very different and more individual types of recall which seemed more directly related to individual autobiographical memory previously stored in the brain (Bloch 1998b). In fact, such accounts should be treated as straightforward linguistic evocations of the past and not assumed to have anything to do with either remembering or recalling.

Such caution is all the more important when we are dealing with accounts of the past created from outside the social group which are foisted on its members, often with ideological intentions, through such mechanisms as formal schooling. Nonetheless, it would be wrong to rule out altogether the possibility of feedback from synchronised evocations of the past on to autobiographical memory. The story of Piaget's watch referred to above is a sign that something of the sort may possibly happen. This may be all the more significant when the individual was not present when the evoked past occurred since the checking of the evocation against possible recollection is not then possible. Thus, in the above mentioned article I describe how in the same village I was shown by a group of Malagasy children where 'they' had hidden during the dreadful repression following the 1947 anti-colonial rebellion in Madagascar. However, none of these children had been born then, yet they seemed to act and speak as though they were recalling their own autobiography. What probably was happening was that the children had been told the story so often that 'we' had hidden in this place that they had come to include themselves in the story and it may have felt as though they remembered the events as having occurred to them (Bloch 1998a). However, whether such accounts are mere rhetorical devices or modifications of memory is not clear and would require further study.

Conclusion

Although there is much more to be said on the topic of memory, there is a way in which the questions it raises and the uncertainty it creates is a good conclusion to this book.

In the first chapter, I noted that the reader may come away with a feeling of knowing less than before. This is totally appropriate. The topic of memory illustrates this. It is one which social scientists particularly like because of its emotional resonance and because it seems to suggest that people are much more the toys of their society or culture than they usually realise. Such argument ought to send a shiver down the spine and at the same time legitimate the centrality of social sciences such as social or cultural anthropology. Yet, as the discussion of the topic of memory suggests, these conclusions are often obtained by means of a lack of critical examination of the vague folk psychology employed. Such a shortcoming introduces a lack of examination of the complexity of the issues involved. This refusal acts as a cover for a much deeper unwillingness. Throughout the book, I have stressed how many anthropologists want to believe that they know about aspects of life of which they can only get minor, though very important, glimpses through the traditional methods of their discipline. Thus, because they can record recallings they assume that these give them access to memory. Because they can record explicit reflexive narratives and observe rituals, they assume that these give them direct access to what it is to be a human being in this or that society. Because they can easily note down words and because they are used to defining these in the way dictionaries do, they claim to be able to access directly the conceptual organisation of the thought processes of the people they study.

These misleading short cuts often lead anthropologists to mistake second-order meta-representations expressed in language or ritual by the people they study for scientifically acceptable analyses of what they indirectly relate to, thereby forgetting that the motivations for the production of such accounts and rituals are quite other than the theoretical intentions of the anthropologist, sociologist or historian. This kind of over-ambition of some anthropological theoretical claims has quite unfairly led to the growing devaluation by many other scholars of the enormous contribution which has been made, and continues to be made, by anthropologists if only it was placed within a wider framework.

Part of the excuse in much anthropology for omitting most aspects of the general process of life is that the history of the discipline has made anthropologists wary of the natural sciences, especially the cognitive sciences. This story from long ago has been a legitimation for surreptitiously making, almost by default, wild psychological assumptions. We saw in chapter 5 examples of this concerning the cognition of time.

Another excuse that anthropologists may give for making what they can observe into an exclusive system is that their methods only allow them to know about what can be easily observed in the field and that they must therefore make do with that. This makes no sense at all. As is the case for any discipline, the limitations of anthropological methods should be a reason for opening doors to different specialities whose different methods give access to what it cannot observe. Falsely making the bits and pieces which anthropologists can easily observe an independent, stand alone system is what has led to the misleading idea of culture in opposition to nature and has legitimated the hostility of social scientists towards natural scientists.

But, if we free ourselves of the notion of a non-natural process which the dark past of the subject anthropology has created, and if we co-operate with other disciplines which also study human beings but in a different way, we can, together, create wider and less tendentious theoretical propositions. When, as a result of such interdisciplinarity, we think together the human physiological, psychological and historical process, we certainly end up with new questions, but these are questions which open up fruitful and manageable avenues for research while at the same time freeing us from blind alleys created by the ghosts of ancient disputes.

References

Anderson, B. 1983. *Imagined Communities Reflections on the Origin and Spread of Nationalism*. London: Verso.

Antze, P. and Lambek, M. 1996. *Tense Past: Cultural Essays in Trauma and Memory*. London: Routledge.

Astuti, R. 2009. 'Revealing and obscuring Rivers's natural pedigrees: biological inheritance and kinship in Madagascar', in J. Leach and S. Bamford (eds.), *Kinship and Beyond: The Genealogical Model Reconsidered*. London: Berghahn, pp. 214–36.

Astuti, R., Solomon, G. and Carey, S. 2004. *Constraints on Conceptual Development*. Monograph of the Society for Research in Child Development, 277, v. 69. Oxford: Blackwell.

Atran, S. 1990. *Cognitive Foundations of Natural history: Towards an Anthropology of Science*. Cambridge University Press.

Austin, J. 1962. *How to Do Things with Words*. Cambridge, MA: Harvard University Press.

Baddeley, A. 1986. *Working Memory*. Oxford University Press.

Baillargeon, R., Kotovsky, L. and Needham, A. 1995. 'The acquisition of physical knowledge in infancy', in D. Sperber, D. Premack and A. J. Premack (eds.), *Causal Cognition*. Oxford University Press, pp. 79–116.

Baillargeon, R., Scott, R. M. and He, Z. 2010. 'False-belief understanding in infants', *Trends in Cognitive Sciences*, 14, pp. 110–18.

Baron-Cohen, S. 2003. *The Essential Difference: Men, Women and the Extreme Male Brain*. London: Penguin/Basic Books.

Bartlett, F. 1932. *Remembering*. Cambridge University Press.

Beteille, A. 1991. *Society and Politics in India: Essays in Comparative Perspective*. London: Athlone.

Bloch, M. 1971. 'The moral and tactical meaning of kinship terms', *Man*, new series, 6 (1), pp. 79–87.

1977. 'The past and the present in the present', *Man*, new series, 12 (2), pp. 278–92.

1985. 'From cognition to ideology', in R. Fardon (ed.), *Power and Knowledge: Anthropological and Sociological Approaches*. Edinburgh: Scottish University Press, pp. 21–48.

1991. 'Language, anthropology and cognitive science', *Man*, new series, 26 (2), pp. 183–98.

1992. 'What goes without saying: the conceptualisation of Zafimaniry society', in A. Kuper (ed.), *Conceptualising Society*. London: Routledge, pp. 127–46.

1998a. 'Autobiographical memory and the historical memory of the more distant past', in M. Bloch (ed.), *How We Think They Think*. Boulder, CO: Westview Press, pp. 114–27.

1998b. 'Time, narratives and the multiplicity of representations of the past', in M. Bloch (ed.), *How We Think They Think*. Boulder, CO: Westview Press, pp. 100–13.

1999. 'Commensality and poisoning', *Social Research*, 66 (1), pp. 133–50.

2001. 'A well-disposed social anthropologist's problem with memes', in Robert Aunger (ed.), *Darwinizing Culture: The Status of Memetics as a Science*. Oxford University Press, pp. 189–204.

2005. 'Where did anthropology go?', in M. Bloch (ed.), *Essays on Cultural Transmission*. London: Berg, pp. 1–20.

2007. 'Durkhemian anthropology and religion: going in and out of each other's bodies', in H. Whitehouse and J. Laidlaw (eds.), *Religion, Anthropology, and Cognitive Science*. Durham, NC: Carolina University Press, pp. 63–80.

2008. 'Why religion is nothing special but is central', *Philosophical Transactions of the Royal Society B: Biological Sciences*, 363 (1499), pp. 2055–61.

Bloch, M. and Sperber, D. 2002. 'Kinship and evolved psychological dispositions: the mother's brother controversy reconsidered', *Current Anthropology*, 43 (4), pp. 723–48.

Bloch, M., Carey, S. and Solomon, G. 2000. 'The development of the understanding of what is passed on from parents to children: a cross cultural investigation', *Cognition and Culture*, 1 (1), pp. 43–68.

Bohannan, L. 1952. 'A genealogical charter', *Africa: Journal of the International African Institute*, 22 (4), pp. 301–15.

Boroditsky, L. 2001. 'Does language shape thought? English and Mandarin speakers' conceptions of time', *Cognitive Psychology*, 43 (1), pp. 1–22.

Botvinick, M. and Cohen, J. 1998. 'Rubber hands "feel" touch that eyes see', *Nature*, 391, p. 756.

Bourdieu, P. 1972. *Esquisse d'une théorie de la pratique*. Paris: Droz.

References

Bower, T. G. R. (1989). *The Rational Infant: Learning in Infancy*. San Francisco: Freeman.

Bowerman, M. and Choi, S. 2003. 'Space under construction: language specific spatial categorisation in first language acquisition', in D. Gentner and S. Goldin-Meadows (eds.), *Language in Mind*. Cambridge, MA: MIT Press, pp. 387–427.

Boyd, R. and Richerson, P. 2005. *The Origin and Evolution of Culture*. Oxford University Press.

Boyer, P. 2009. 'Extending the range of adaptive misbelief: memory "distortions" as functional features', *Behavioral and Brain Sciences*, 32 (6), pp. 513–14.

Brown, R. 1973. *A First Language: The Early Stages*. Cambridge, MA: Harvard University Press.

Bullock, M. and Gelman, R. 1979. 'Preschool children's assumptions about cause and effect: temporal ordering', *Child Development*, 50, pp. 89–96.

Butler, J. 1993. *Bodies That Matter: On the Discursive Limits of 'Sex'*. London: Routledge.

Carey, S. 1991. 'Knowledge acquisition or conceptual change?', in S. Carey and S. Gelman (eds.), *The Epigenesis of Mind: Essays on Biology and Cognition*. Hillsdale, NJ: L. Erlbaum, pp. 133–69.

    2009. *The Origin of Concepts*. Oxford University Press.

Carey, S. and Spelke, E. 1994. 'Domain-specific knowledge and conceptual change', in L. Hirshfeld and S. Gelman (eds.), *Mapping the Mind: Domain Specificity in Cognition and Culture*. Cambridge University Press, pp. 169–200.

Carsten, J. 1995. 'The politics of forgetting: migration kinship and memory in a Malay fishing community', *Journal of the Royal Anthropological Institute*, new series, 1, pp. 317–35.

Certeau de, M. 1980. *Art de faire, I: L'invention du quotidien*. Paris: Gallimard.

Cheney, D. and Sefarth, R. 2007. *Baboon Metaphysics*. Chicago University Press.

Christian, W. 1998. 'L'œil de l'esprit. Les visionnaires basques en transe, 1931, *Terrain*, 30, pp. 5–22.

Church, R. M. and Gibbon, J. 1982. 'Temporal generalization', *Journal of Experimental Psychology: Animal Behavior Processes*, 8, pp. 165–86.

Clayton, N. S. and Russell, J. 2009. 'Looking for episodic memory in animals and young children: prospects for a new minimalism', *Neuropsychologia*, 47, pp. 2330–40.

Cole, M. 1996. *Cultural Psychology*. Cambridge, MA: Harvard University Press.

Colier, J. and Yanagisako, S. 1987. *Gender and Kinship: Towards a Unified Analysis*. Stanford University Press.

Connerton, P. *How Societies Remember*. Cambridge University Press.

Conway, M. 2001. 'Sensory-perceptual episodic memory and its context: autobiographical memory', *Philosophical Transactions of the Royal Society Series B*, pp. 1375–84.

Conway, M. A. 2005. 'Memory and the self', *Journal of Memory and Language*, 53 (4), pp. 594–628.

Cosmides, L., Tooby, J. and Barkow, J. (1992). 'Evolutionary psychology and conceptual integration', in J. Barkow, L. Cosmides and J. Tooby (eds.), *The Adapted Mind: Evolutionary Psychology and the Generation of Culture*. Oxford University Press, pp. 3–18.

Cunnison, I. 1960. *The Luapula Peoples of Northern Rhodesia: Custom and History in Tribal Politics*. Manchester University Press.

Damasio, A. 1999. *The Feeling of What Happens*. London: Heineman.

D'Andrade, R. 1995. *The Development of Cognitive Anthropology*. Cambridge University Press.

David, N., Newen, A. and Vogeley, K. 2008. 'The "sense of agency" and its underlying cognitive and neural mechanisms', *Consiousness and Cognition*, 17 (2), pp. 523–34.

Dawkins, R. 1976. *The Selfish Gene*. Oxford University Press.

1982. *The Extended Phenotype*. Oxford University Press.

Decety, J. 2010. 'The neurodevelopment of empathy in humans', *Developmental Neuroscience*, 32, pp. 257–67.

Degler, C. 1991. *In Search of Human Nature*. New York: Oxford University Press.

Dennett, D. 1991. *Consciousness Explained*. Boston, MA: Little Brown.

1992. 'The self as a centre of narrative gravity', in F. Kessel, P. Cole and D. Johnson (eds.), *Self and Consciousness: Multiple Perspectives*. Hillsdale, NJ: L. Erlbaum, pp. 103–15.

1995. *Darwin's Dangerous Idea*. London: Penguin.

Derrida, J. 1967. *De la gramatologie*. Paris: Édition de Minuit.

Donnelly, P. and Foley, R. (eds.) 2001. *Genes, Fossils and Behaviour: An Integrated Approach to Human Evolution*. Brussels: NATO.

Dumont, L. 1983. *Essais sur l'individualisme*. Paris: Seuil.

Dunbar, R. 1997. *Grooming, Gossip and the Evolution of Language*. Cambridge, MA: Harvard University Press.

Durham, W. 1991. *Coevolution*. Stanford University Press.

Durkheim, E. 1893. *La division du travail social*. Paris: Felix Alcan.

1912; 1960. *Les formes élémentaires de la vie religieuse*. Paris: Alcan; PUF: Paris.

Emery, N. and Clayton, N. 2004. 'The mentality of crows: convergent evolution of intelligence in corvids and apes', *Science*, 306, no. 5703, pp. 1903–7.

Enfield, N. and Levinson, S. (eds.) 2006. *Roots of Human Sociality*. Oxford: Berg.

References

Evans-Pritchard, E. 1940. *The Nuer*. Oxford University Press.

Ewing, K. 1990. 'The illusion of wholeness: culture, self and the experience of inconsistency', *Ethnos*, 18 (3), pp. 251–78.

Farrer, C. and Frith, C. 2002. 'Experiencing oneself vs another person as being the cause of an action: the neural correlates of the experience of agency', *Neuroimage*, 15 (3), pp. 596–603.

Fillmore, C. 1971. 'Types of lexical information', in D. Steinberg and L. Jakobovits (eds.), *Semantics: An Interdisciplinary Reader*. Cambridge University Press, pp. 370–87.

Fodor, J. 1980. 'On the impossibility of acquiring more powerful structures', in Massimo Piattelli-Palmarini (ed.), *Language and Learning: The Debate Between Jean Piaget and Noam Chomsky*. Cambridge, MA: Harvard University Press, 142–63.

Freeman, D. 1983. *Margaret Mead and Samoa: The Making and Unmaking of an Anthropological Myth*. Cambridge, MA: Harvard University Press.

Friedman, W. 1990. 'Children's representations of the pattern of daily activities', *Child Development*, 61, pp. 1399–412.

Gallup, G. 1970. 'Chimpanzees: self-recognition', *Science*, 167, pp. 86–7.

Geertz, C. 1973. *The Interpretation of Cultures*. New York: Basic Books.

Gellner, E. 1998. *Language and Solitude: Wittgenstein, Malinowski, and the Habsburg Dilemma*. Cambridge University Press.

Giddens, A. 1981. *A Contemporary Critique of Historical Materialism*, I. Berkeley: University of California Press.

Goody, E. 1978. 'Towards a theory of questions', in E. Goody (ed.), *Questions and Politeness*. Cambridge University Press, pp. 17–43.

Gow, P. 2001. *An Amazonian Myth and Its History*. Oxford University Press.

Grice, H. 1968. 'Utterer's meaning, sentence meaning and word meaning', *Foundations of Language*, 4, pp. 1–18.

Hacking, I. 1996. 'Memory sciences, memory politics', in P. Antze and M. Lambek (eds.), *Tense Past*. New York: Routledge, pp. 67–88.

Halbwachs, M. 1925. *Les cadres sociaux de la mémoire*. Paris: Alcan. Translated as *On Collective Memory* by L. Coser, Chicago University Press, 1992.

Harris, P. 2000. *The Work of the Imagination*. Oxford: Blackwell.

Harris, P. and Kavanaugh, R. 1993. *Young Children's Understanding of Pretense*. Monographs of the Society for Research in Child Development, vol. 58, no. 1.

Hauser, M. 2006. *Moral Minds: How Nature Designed our Universal Sense of Right and Wrong*. New York: Harper Collins.

Hauser, M., Kralik, J., Botto-Mahan, C., Garrett, M. and Oser, J. 1995. 'Self-recognition in primates: phylogeny and the salience of species-typical features',

Proceedings of the National Academy of Sciences of the United States of America, 92 (23), pp. 10811–14.

Holland, D. and Quinn, N. 1997. *Cultural Models in Language and Thought.* Cambridge University Press.

Horton, R. 1970. 'African traditional thought and western science', in Bryan Wilson (ed.), *Rationality.* Oxford: Blackwell, pp. 131–71.

Humphrey, N. 2007. 'The society of selves', *Philosophical Transactions of the Royal Society. B*, 362, pp. 745–54.

Humphrey, N. and Dennett, D. 1989. 'Speaking for ourselves: an assessment of multiple personality disorder', *Raritan*, 9 (1), pp. 68–98.

Ingold, T. 2000. *The Perception of the Environment: Essays on Livelihood, Dwelling and Skill.* London: Routledge.

Johnson, M. 1988. 'Memories of mother', *New Scientist*, 18, pp. 60–2.

Johnson-Laird, P. 1983. *Mental models.* Cambridge University Press.

Karmiloff-Smith, A. 1999. *Beyond Modularity: A Developmental Perspective on Cognitive Science.* Cambridge, MA: MIT Press.

Keil, F. 1989. *Concepts, Kinds and Cognitive Development.* Cambridge, MA: MIT Press.

Knoblich, G. and Sebanz, N. 2008. 'Evolving intentions for social interactions: from entrainment to joint action', *Philosophical Transactions of the Royal Society*, Series B, 363, pp. 2021–2031 (also publ. in C. Renfrew, C. Frith and L. Malafouris (eds.), *The Sapient Mind: Archaeology Meets Neuroscience*, Oxford 2009).

Kondo, D. K. 1990. *Crafting Selves.* Chicago University Press.

Konvalinka, I. et al. 2011. 'Synchronized arousal between performers and related spectators in a fire-walking ritual', *Proceedings of the National Academy of Sciences of the USA*, 108 (20), pp. 8514–19.

Kuper, A. 1999. *Culture: The Anthropologists' Account.* Cambridge, MA: Harvard University Press.

Landes, D. 1998. *The Wealth and Poverty of Nations.* New York: Norton.

Langoenden, D. 1968. *The London School of Linguistics.* Cambridge, MA: MIT Press.

Laqueur, T. 1990. *Making Sex: Body and Gender from the Greeks to Freud.* Cambridge, MA: Harvard University Press.

Latour, B. 2005. *Reassembling the Social: An Introduction to Actor-Network Theory.* Oxford University Press.

Latour, B. and Woolgar, S. 1979. *Laboratory Life: The Social Construction of Scientific Facts.* Princeton University Press.

Lave, J. and Wenger, E. 1991. *Situated Learning.* Cambridge University Press.

Leach, E. 1954. *Political Systems of Highland Burma.* London: Bell.

　1966. 'Virgin birth', *Proceedings of the Royal Anthropological Institute of Great Britain and Ireland*, pp. 39–49.

References

Leenhardt, G. 1985. 'Self: public, private, some African representations', in M. Carrithers, S. Collins and S. Lukes (eds.), *The Category of the Person*. Cambridge University Press, pp. 141–55.

Levinson, S. 1983. *Pragmatics*. Cambridge University Press.

    2003. *Space in Language and Cognition: Explorations in Cognitive Diversity*. Cambridge University Press.

Lévi-Strauss, C. 1958. *Anthropologie Structurale*. Paris: Plon.

    1962. *Le totémisme aujourd'hui*. Paris: Presses Universitaires de France.

Lounsbury, F. 1964. 'The structural analysis of kinship semantics', *Proceedings of the Ninth International Congress of Linguistics* (reprinted in S. Tyler (ed.), *Cognitive Anthropology*, New York: Holt Rinehart and Wilson, pp. 193–212).

Lucy, J. A. 1992. *Language Diversity and Thought*. Cambridge University Press.

Malinowski, B. 1922. *Argonauts of the Western Pacific*. London: Routledge.

    1925. *Magic, Science and Religion*. London: Routledge.

    1926. *Myth in Primitive Psychology*. London: Psyche Miniatures.

    1935. *The Language of Magic and Gardening* (*Coral Gardens and their Magic*, ii). London: Allen and Unwin.

Malotki, E. 1983. *Hopi Time: A Linguistic Analysis of the Temporal Categories in Hopi Language*. Berlin: Mouton.

Markus, H. and Kitiyama, S. 1991. 'Culture and the self: implications for cognition, emotion and motivation', *Psychological Review*, 98 (2), pp. 224–53.

Marriott, McK. and Inden, R. 1977. 'Towards an ethnosociology of South Indian caste systems', in D. Kenneth (ed.), *The New Wind: Changing Identities*. The Hague: Mouton, pp. 227–38.

Mauss, M. 1906. 'Les variations saisonnières des sociétés Eskimos: essai de morphologie sociale', *L'Année Sociologique*, 12 (1904–5), pp. 39–132.

    1923–4. 'Essai sur le don', *L'Année Sociologique*, 1, pp. 30–186.

    1924. 'Rapports réels et pratiques de la sociologie et de la psychologie', *Journal de Psychologie Normale et Pathologique*, pp. 892–310.

    1935. 'Les techniques du corps', *Journal de Psychologie Normale et Pathologique*, pp. 271–93.

    1938. 'Une catégorie de l'esprit humain: la notion de personne, celle du "moi", un plan de travail', *Journal of the Royal Anthropological Institute*, 68, pp. 263–81.

    1985. 'A category of the human mind: the notion of the person: the notion of self', in M. Carrithers, S. Collins and S. Lukes (eds.), *The Category of the Person*. Cambridge University Press, pp. 1–25.

Mead, M. 1935. *Sex and Temperament in Three Primitive Societies*. New York: Harper Collins.

    1949. *Male and Female*. New York: Harper Collins.

Medin, D. and Ortony, A. 1989. 'Psychological essentialism', in S. Vosniadou and A. Ortony (eds.), *Similarity and Analogical Reasoning*. New York: Cambridge University Press, pp. 179–95.

Medin, D. and Schaffer, M. 1978. 'Context theory of classification learning', *Psychological Review*, 85 (3), pp. 207–38.

Montagu, Ashley 1942. *Man's Most Dangerous Myth: The Fallacy of Race*. Walnut Creek, CA: Alta Mira Press.

Moore, C. and Lemmon, K. 2001. *The Self in Time: Developmental Perspectives*. Hillsdale, NJ: L. Erlbaum.

Morgan, L. 1871. 'Systems of consanguinity and affinity of the human family', *Smithsonian Contributions to Knowledge*, 17, pp. 4–602.

Morris, M., Nisbett, R. and Peng, K. 1995. 'Causal attribution across domains and cultures', in D. Sperber, D. Premack and A. Premack, *Causal Cognition*. Oxford University Press, pp. 613–15.

Munn, N. 1983. 'Gawan Kula: spatiotemporal control and the symbolism of influence', in J. Leach and E. Leach (eds.), *The Kula: New Perspective on Massim Exchange*. Cambridge University Press, pp. 277–308.

1986. *The Fame of Gawa*. Chicago University Press.

Murphy, G. and Medin, D. 1985. 'The role of theories in conceptual coherence', *Psychological Review*, 92 (3), pp. 289–316.

Nakamura, K., Kawashima, R. and Sato, N. et al. 2000. 'Functional delineation of the human occipito-temporal areas related to face and scene processing. A PET study', *Brain*, 123 (9), pp. 1903–12.

Needham, R. 1971. 'Remarks on the analysis of kinship and marriage', in R. Needham (ed.), *Rethinking Kinship and Marriage*. London: Tavistock, pp. 1–34.

Neisser, U. 1988. 'Five kinds of self knowledge', *Philosophical Psychology*, 1, pp. 35–59.

Nelson, K. 1986. 'Event knowledge and cognitive development', in K. Nelson (ed.), *Event Knowledge: Structure and Function in Development*. Hillsdale, NJ: L. Erlbaum.

2003. 'Narrative and self, myth and memory: emergence of the cultural self', in R. Fivush and C. Haden (eds.), *Autobiographical Memory and the Construction of a Narrative Self*. Mahwah, NJ: L. Erlbaum, pp. 3–28.

Nora, P. 1984. *Les lieux de mémoire*. Paris: NRF Galimard.

O'Connell, B. and Gerard, A. 'Scripts and scraps: the development of sequential understanding', *Child Development*, 56, pp. 671–81.

Ortner, S. 1973. 'On key symbols', *American Anthropologist*, 75, pp. 1338–46.

1974. 'Is female to male as nature is to culture?', in M. Z. Rosaldo and L. Lamphere (eds.), *Woman, Culture and Society*. Stanford University Press.

References

Ortner, S. and Whitehead, H. 1981. *Sexual Meanings: The Cultural Construction of Gender and Sexuality*. Cambridge University Press.

Parry, J. 1989. 'The end of the body', in M. Feher, R. Naddaff and G. Tazi (eds.), *Fragments for a History of the Body*, II. New York: Zone Books, pp. 490–517.

Parry, J. 1991. 'The Hindu lexicographer? A note on auspiciousness and purity', *Contributions to Indian Sociology*, n.s. 25 (2), pp. 267–85.

Piaget, J. 1962. *Plays, Dreams and Imitation in Childhood*. New York: Norton.

  1968. *Le structuralisme*. Paris: PUF.

  1969. *The Mechanisms of Perception*. London: Routledge and Kegan Paul.

Piette, A. 2009. *Propositions anthropologiques pour refondre la discipline*. Paris: Petra.

Pinker, S. 1995. *The Language Instinct*. London: Penguin Books.

  2002. *The Blank Slate*. London: Allen Lane.

Quine, W. 1969. 'Epistemology naturalized', in *Ontological Relativity and Other Essays*. New York: Columbia University Press, pp. 69–90.

Quinn, N. 2006. 'The self', *Anthropological Theory*, 6 (3), pp. 365–87.

Radcliffe-Brown, A. and Forde, D. 1950. *African Systems of Kinship and Marriage*. Oxford University Press.

Rakoczy, H. 2008. 'Pretence as individual and collective intentionality', *Mind and Language*, 23 (5), pp. 499–517.

Rakoczy, H. and Tomasello, M. 2006. 'Two-year-olds grasp the intentional structure of pretense acts', *Developmental Science*, 9 (6), pp. 557–64.

Regnier, D. Forthcoming. 'Why not marry them? History, essentialism, and the discrimination against slave descendants in the southern highlands of Madagascar'.

Ricoeur, P. 1985. *Temps et Récit*, III. Paris: Seuil.

Rizzolatti, G. et al. 1996. 'Premotor cortex and the recognition of motor actions', *Cognitive Brain Research*, 3, pp. 131–41.

Rosaldo, M. and Lamphere, L. (eds.) 1974. *Women, Culture and Society*. Stanford University Press.

Rosaldo, M. Z. 1984. 'Towards an anthropology of self and feeling', in R. Schweder and R. LeVine (eds.), *Culture Theory*. Cambridge University Press, pp. 137–57.

Rosch, E. 1973. 'Natural categories', *Cognitive Psychology*, 4, pp. 328–50.

Rosch, E. and Mervis, C. 1975. 'Family resemblances: studies in the internal structure of categories', *Cognitive Psychology*, 7, pp. 573–605.

Rose, D. 1980. 'Malinowski's influence on Wittgenstein on the matter of *use* in language', *Journal of the History of the Behavioral Sciences*, 16 (2), pp. 145–9.

Russell, J., Alexis, D. and Clayton, N. 2010. 'Episodic future thinking in 3- to 5-year-old-children: the ability to think of what will be needed from a different point of view', *Cognition*, 114 (1), pp. 56–71.

Sahlins, M. 1977. *The Use and Abuse of Biology: An Anthropological Critique of Socio-biology*. Ann Arbor: University of Michigan Press.

Schneider, D. 1984. *A Critique of the Study of Kinship*. Chicago University Press.

Searle, J. 1969. *Speech Acts: An Essay in the Philosophy of Language*. Cambridge University Press.

1995. *The Construction of Social Reality*. New York: Free Press.

Seeley, W. and Sturm, V. 2006. 'Self representation and the frontal lobes', in B. Miller and J. Cummings (eds.), *The Human Frontal Lobes*, 2nd edn. New York: Guilford Press, pp. 317–34.

Schank, R. and Abelson, R. 1977. *Scripts, Plans Goals and Understanding*. Hillsdale NJ: L. Erlbaum.

Skowronski, J. and Sedikides, C. 2007. 'Temporal knowledge and autobiographical memory: an evolutionary perspective', in R. Dunbar and L. Barrett (eds.), *Oxford Handbook of Evolutionary Psychology*. Oxford University Press, pp. 505–17.

Slobin, D. I. 1991. 'Learning to think for speaking: native language, cognition, and rhetorical style', *Pragmatics*, 1, pp. 7–26.

Snell, B. 1953. *The Discovery of the Mind*, trans. T. G. Rosenmeyer. Cambridge, MA: Harvard University Press.

Spelke, E. 1988. 'The origins of physical knowledge', in L. Weitzkrantz (ed.), *Thought Without Language*. Oxford University Press, pp. 168–84.

Spelke, E., Philips, A. and Woodward, A. 1995. 'Infant's knowlwdge of object motion and human action', in D. Sperber, D. Premack and A. Premack (eds.), *Causal Cognition*. Oxford University Press, pp. 44–78.

Sperber, D. 1982. *Le savoir des anthropologues*. Paris: Hermann.

1985. 'Anthropology and psychology: towards an epidemiology of representations', *Man*, n.s. 20, pp. 73–89.

1996. *Explaining Culture: A Naturalistic Approach*. Oxford: Blackwell.

2000. 'Metarepresentations in an evolutionary perspective', in *Metarepresentations: A Multidisciplinary Approach*. Oxford University Press, pp. 117–38.

2001. 'An objection to the memetic approach to culture', in R. Aunger (ed.), *Darwinizing Culture: The Status of Memetics as a Science*. Cambridge University Press, pp. 163–74.

Sperber, D. and Wilson, D. 1986. *Relevance*. Oxford: Blackwell.

Spiro, M. 1993. 'Is the western conception of the self "peculiar" within the context of the world cultures', *Ethos*, 21 (2), pp. 107–53.

Squire, L.R. 1992. 'Memory and the hippocampus: a synthesis from findings with monkeys and humans', *Psychological Reviews*, 99 (2), pp. 195–231.

Stocking, G. 1968. *Race, Culture and Evolution*. New York: Free Press.

1987. *Victorian Anthropology*. New York: Free Press.

References

Strathern, M. 1988. *The Gender of the Gift*. Berkeley: University of California Press.

Strauss, C. and Quinn, N. 1997. *A Cognitive Theory of Cultural Meaning*. Cambridge University Press.

Strawson, G. 1999. 'The self and the SESMET', in S. Gallagher and J. Shear (eds.), *Models of the Self*. Thorverton: Imprint Academic, pp. 99–135.

2005. 'Against narrativity', in G. Strawson (ed.), *The Self?* Oxford: Blackwell, pp. 63–86.

Suddendorf, T. and Corballis, M. C. 1997. 'Mental time travel and the evolution of the human mind', *Genetic, Social, and General Psychology Monographs*, 123, pp. 133–67.

Tomasello, M. 1999. *The Cultural Origins of Human Cognition*. Cambridge University Press.

2009. *Why We Cooperate*. Cambridge, MA: MIT Press.

Tooby, J. and Cosmides, L. 1992. 'Psychological foundations of culture', in J. Barkow, L. Cosmides and J. Tooby (eds.), *The Adapted Mind: Evolutionary Psychology and the Generation of Culture*. Oxford University Press, pp. 19–136.

Trouillot, M.-R. 1995. *Silencing the Past*. Boston: Beacon Press.

Tulving, E. 1972. 'Episodic and semantic memory', in E. Tulving and W. Donaldson (eds.), *Organization of Memory*. New York: Academic Press, pp. 382–402.

1985. 'Memory and consciousness', *Canadian Psychology*, 26, pp. 1–12.

Tyler, S. (ed.) 1969. *Cognitive Anthropology*. New York: Holt, Rinehart and Winston.

Valentine Daniel, E. 1984. *Fluid Signs: Being a Person the Tamil Way*. Berkeley: California University Press.

Vogeley, K. and Fink, G. 2003. 'Neural correlates of the first-person-perspective', *Trends in Cognitive Science*, 7 (1), pp. 38–42.

Wallace, A. 1965. 'The problem of the psychological validity of componential analysis', *American Anthropologist*, 67 (5), part 2, pp. 229–48.

Waxman, S. and Booth, A. 2003. 'Mapping words to the world in infancy: infants' expectations for count nouns and adjectives', *Journal of Cognition and Development*, 4 (3), pp. 357–81.

Whiten, A. and Suddendorf, T. (2007). 'Great ape cognition and the evolutionary roots of human imagination', in I. Roth (ed.), *Imaginative Minds*. London: Oxford University Press, pp. 31–60.

Whorf, B. L. 1941. 'The relation of habitual thought and behaviour to language', in L. Spier (ed.), *Language, Culture and Personality*. Menasha: Sapir Memorial Publication Fund, pp. 134–59.

1964. *Language, Thought and Reality*. Cambridge, MA: MIT Press.

Wikan, U. 1990. *Managing Turbulent Hearts*. University of Chicago Press.

Williams, H. and Conway, M. 2009. 'Networks of autobiographical memories', in P. Boyer and J. Wertsch (eds.), *Memory in Mind and Culture*. Cambridge University Press, pp. 33–61.

Wilson, E. O. 1975. *Sociobiology: The New Synthesis*. Cambridge, MA: Harvard University Press.

Wittgenstein, L. 1953. *Philosophical Investigations*, trans. G. E. M. Anscombe. Oxford: Blackwell.

Wood, J. 2008. *How Fiction Works*. New York: Farrar.

Woodburn, J. 1982. 'Egalitarian Societies', *Man*, n.s. 17 (3), pp. 431–51.

Zahavi, D. n.d. 'Minimal self and narrative self: a distinction in need of refinement', unpublished manuscript.

Index

Index

Index